In the Spirit of Truth

In the Spirit of Truth

A reader in the work of Frank Lake

Introduction by David Lyall

Edited by CAROL CHRISTIAN

Darton, Longman and Todd
London

First published in 1991 by
Darton, Longman and Todd Ltd
89 Lillie Road, London SW6 1UD

British Library Cataloguing in Publication Data
Lake, Frank, *1914–1982*
    In the spirit of truth: a reader in the work of Frank
    Lake.
    1. Christianity: Pastoral Work
    I. Title II. Christian, Carol
    253.5

ISBN 0–232–51931–5

Phototypeset by Input Typesetting Ltd, London SW19 8DR
Printed and bound by Courier International Ltd, Tiptree, Essex

Contents

Acknowledgements

My deep appreciation is due to Peter van de Kasteele, General Director of the Clinical Theology Association, St Mary's House, Church Westcote, Oxford, who, following Darton, Longman and Todd's suggestion that such a book might be welcome, invited me to take on the job of bringing it into being. He has fed me with suggestions and material, read the manuscript at various stages, and been its sponsor. Also to Patricia van de Kasteele for encouragement and clarification of certain points. To Sylvia Lake for friendly support, and for facing the risk of seeing Frank's work reshaped, as it were, in other hands than his. Two points which she 'should have liked to put to him if he were here', are included in the notes. A big thank you to Martin Yeomans for reading the typescript for errors, for answering queries, and for helpful comment; and to Roger Moss for checking the section on the Maternal-Foetal Syndrome. Grateful thanks to my husband John who has been my mainstay throughout.

Thanks to those who have sent me articles or tapes which they valued: Richard Dupuis, Bill Hammond Smith, John Michael Hughes, Len Wigg. I owe my own education in Clinical Theology mainly to Dennis Hyde and Tony Waite, with whom I have shared the running of CT seminars.

I acknowledge with thanks permission to reprint extracts from the following sources: The Clinical Theology Association for materials from the Lingdale Archive; Darton, Longman and Todd Ltd for Frank Lake's *Clinical Theology* and *Tight Corners in Pastoral Counselling*; The BBC Third Programme, for 'What is Clinical Theology?', 'Images of God' and 'Lighten Our Darkness'; *Contact* magazine, for 'The care of the anxious', 'Hope in the clinical setting', 'The newer therapies', 'Reflection on development and change in the Clinical Theology Association 1964–1975' and 'The theology of pastoral counselling'; *The Epworth Review*, for 'The emotional health of the clergy'; T & T Clark Ltd, publishers of *The Expository Times*, for articles from their series First Aid in Counselling: 'The threatened nervous breakdown' Parts 1 and 2, and 'The homosexual man'; Hodder and Stoughton, publishers of *We Must Love One Another or Die*, editor Hugh Montefiore, for 'The sexual aspects of personality'; *New Statesman and Society*, for 'Casework theology' by Michael Hare Duke; the Post Green Community, in Lytchett Minster, Dorset, for the transcript of CT seminars held there; *Renewal* magazine for articles under the heading 'Frank Lake Replies': 'I don't want to feel angry but I do', 'More about anger: is it or isn't it sin?', 'I just feel worthless', 'Same-sex loving' Parts 1 and 2; Unwin Hyman Ltd, for extracts from Frank Lake's Foreword and Appendix to *A Christian Therapy for a Neurotic World*, by E. N. Ducker.

Attempts have been made to ascertain whether several of the typescripts in the Lingdale Archive, written with publication in mind, were indeed published. If so, the editor would be glad to hear from the copyright holders, so that due acknowledgement can be made in future editions of this book.

Preface

Frank Lake's Christian mission was to heal the individual in body, mind and spirit. From his days as a doctor in India, through his ministry as a psychiatrist in England (frequently to those who were themselves ministers) through his later years of search for the synthesis between the disciplines of psychology and theology which became known as Clinical Theology, his words, spoken and written, have had a powerful, often decisive, impact on the lives of many people. Since I embarked on this project, a number of them have taken the trouble to say just that: *What I heard/read changed my life.*

For this reason his publishers suggested the gathering together into a 'Reader' of some of the material originating with him – drawing on lectures, articles, sermons, newsletters (to the membership of the Clinical Theology Association of which he was Director) and tapescripts of seminars and conferences led by him – mostly things not previously published in book form.

Inevitably it is only a selection. Nor does it break new ground. But Frank had the happy knack of re-rehearsing his ideas in fresh ways, instilling the same teaching in different guises, finding new connections, discovering new facets in a previously used image, repeating himself much less often than would seem possible for one who wrote constantly, swiftly and, as he himself ruefully admitted, at very great length indeed. Even those deeply imbued with his philosophy may, I hope, have that happy 'Aha!' experience as they come upon a paragraph or page that brings some previously obscure proposition to life and recognize his distinctive voice.

A selection, though I have tried to make it representative, is necessarily personal, especially when space is limited. Frank Lake's writings form a yeasty religious-psychological brew which I, as a laywoman of a somewhat sceptical cast of mind, can only judge by whether or not they 'hit the spot'. I feel that I have been inspired, instructed, and perhaps even, in my innermost being, transformed, by my contacts with the Clinical Theology movement. But when the brew boils up into a froth of ideas either incomprehensible or untenable to me, I can only skim it off, hoping that I have not, thereby, distorted his meaning! Another might – and may in future – conserve what I have discarded.

I conceive of this 'Reader' as meeting the needs of several groups of people: those who would like an introduction to Clinical Theology; those who, having passed through at least two years of seminars at some time, would welcome a reminder of ideas they may not have fully absorbed; those who, in their day-to-day giving of themselves in care for other people, may find – or may always have found – in the words of Frank Lake a life-renewing source of acceptance, sustenance, and of mental and spiritual stimulation. Others (and for them an index is included) may find it helpful for clarifying specific situations or problems, for pointing a way through the haziness that affects anyone attempting to sort out human relationships.

CAROL CHRISTIAN

Note

Square brackets in the readings denote editorial interpolation, in roman type for missing words or phrases, in italic for explanations or comments. Italic type is also used for words which Frank Lake himself stressed in his writings or talks and so, I hope, reflects his voice.

Introduction: Clinical Theology in Context

In 1966 Frank Lake's *Clinical Theology*,[1] was published. This was a massive tome of over 1000 pages whose contents reflected the creative mind and the spirituality of a man who has made his own uniquely significant contribution to pastoral care and education in Britain. It will come as no surprise that Dr Lake was the prolific author of many other papers and lectures. Twenty-five years after that first major publication is perhaps an appropriate time to explore the significance of these occasional papers for pastoral ministry in the 1990s. For this reason Carol Christian's collecting and editing of them is to be warmly welcomed.

The purpose of this introduction is simple. It is to set Clinical Theology in the context of the radical transformation in our understanding of the pastoral task which has taken place within the past generation. For not only did Frank Lake write a big book: he was a person, as enigmatic as he was charismatic, whose ideas launched a movement which has in varying degrees influenced the thought and the practice of many thousands of people involved in pastoral ministry, both ordained and lay.

Frank Lake's original intention was to create a system of in-service pastoral training for the clergy and one must realize how necessary this was when he began this task in the late 1950s. Ministers were trained in universities and theological colleges. In English universities, pastoral care did not feature within the theological disciplines and even in the ancient Scottish universities, with their Professors of Practical Theology, the subject was not taught as part of the B.D. degree, but was an additional 'church' subject, being considered of low academic significance. When 'pastoralia' was taught (in England this was done within the theological colleges) it was of a distinctly 'helpful hints and tips' variety with little theoretical or even theological rootage.

The 1960s saw a number of new developments in pastoral care and counselling in Britain. In 1959, the Scottish Pastoral Association (SPA) had been formed, seeking to bring into dialogue ministers, doctors and social workers. This was followed in 1960 by the first issue of the SPA's journal, *Contact*. Frank Lake lectured at the SPA Annual Conference in St Andrews in 1962 (my first experience of his famous charts!) and soon, together with the recently-formed and London-based Institute of Religion and Medicine, the Clinical Theology Association began to share in the sponsorship of *Contact*. This was also the era of the post-Robbins expansion in higher education, making it possible for some universities to introduce Diplomas in Pastoral Studies, e.g. at St Andrews (James Whyte), Edinburgh (James Blackie) and Birmingham (Bob Lambourne). The teaching of Pastoral Studies in the theological colleges was heavily influenced by an important report produced jointly by the Institute of Religion and Medicine and the British Council of Churches.[2] Certain Anglican dioceses began to appoint Advisers in Pastoral Care and Counselling. Finally, one or two centres for pastoral counselling and training were founded, such as the Westminster Pastoral Foundation by William Kyle and the Dympna Centre by Father Louis Marteau.

How can one account for this explosion of interest in pastoral care and counselling? A number of factors were probably significant. First of all the 'new psychology' began to exert an influence which was both direct and indirect. Directly, a number of Christian ministers had realized that one did not have to accept Freud's philosophical views about religion in order to appreciate the significance for pastoral ministry of his understanding of the growth of human personality and the dynamics of personal relationships. Oscar Pfister,[3] J. G. McKenzie,[4] Leslie Weatherhead[5] and Harry Guntrip[6] were pioneers in this exploration. Most significant for the present discussion, Guntrip was one of Frank Lake's teachers at Leeds where he studied for a Diploma in Psychological Medicine on returning from India. Guntrip was one of those who espoused an 'Object-Relations Theory' of human personality postulated by W. D. Fairbairn[7] and others. This theory moved significantly beyond Freud's model of human growth and development based upon instinctive drives to one which rooted personality development in the quality of the relationship between mother and child – an idea which was to become the lynch-pin of all of Frank Lake's future work.

Indirectly, new understandings of personhood were beginning to inform the theoretical framework and practice of other caring professions such as psychiatry, social work and the increasing number of counselling organizations, e.g. the Marriage Guidance

Council (now Relate), and in such a culture pastoral ministry could not but be influenced by fresh insights into the nature of helping relationships. Finally, the rapidly expanding pastoral counselling movement in North America began to make its impact in Europe both through familiarity with the literature and through Europeans crossing the Atlantic for periods of study. (Bill Kyle set up the Westminster Pastoral Foundation after spending some time in the United States.)

Thus the Clinical Theology Association began to flourish in the 1960s as part of a network of people and organizations committed to the development of pastoral care and counselling (a network which in time became the Association for Pastoral Care and Counselling). A pattern of three-hour training sessions was established, held every three weeks over a period of two years. Frank produced pamphlets for the seminars as well as the amazingly complex charts which together developed into *Clinical Theology*; tutors were trained; first clergymen of the Church of England, then ministers and lay people of other denominations, participated in the seminars in increasing numbers.

What did the participants gain from the experience? Reflection on my own experience of one group suggests several factors. First, there was the support of the group and the realization that within other congregations there were colleagues who were also coping with people who were depressed or afflicted by hysteric, schizoid or paranoid reaction patterns; second, an understanding of the person, for Clinical Theology did provide a conceptual framework for thinking about what was happening to people; third, a milieu in which a degree of self-understanding became possible; fourth, an introduction to what were then new secular contributions to understanding and caring for people such as Transactional Analysis and Gestalt Therapy – such was Frank's eclecticism; fifth, the development of some pastoral skills which could be used in ministry; and finally, a way of integrating a psychological with a theological understanding of the person.

Clinical Theology has never been universally accepted either by theologians or psychiatrists. While many found value in the system which sought to integrate theological and psychological understandings of the person, it must be recognized that it is really an attempt to relate a fairly narrow range of theological perspectives with an equally limited part of the spectrum of psychological insight. In the first volume of essays entitled *Religion and Medicine*, the editor Hugh Melinsky writes of Clinical Theology:

For theological guidance, Dr Lake looks principally to Job, St John's Gospel, St Paul's Epistle to the Romans, Kirkegaard, Simone Weil and Martin Buber. His psychological mentors are Freud and the neo-Freudians, Klein, Fairbairn, Sullivan and Guntrip. Since there are great divergences amongst theologians and psychiatrists in their own fields, it is hardly to be expected that any one mortal could lead these two contentious disciplines to a happy marriage.[8]

Later Melinsky adds:

There are many flashes of insight sparked off by the high tension contact between the fields of theology and psychiatry. But there are also links made between the two disciplines which are too simple.[9]

Even more contentious was Frank's later emphasis upon the 'Maternal-Foetal Distress Syndrome', his assertion that the roots of much human mental pain could be traced to the impact upon the foetus of events which took place in the life of the mother during the first three months of pregnancy. This controversy was brought into sharp focus by Alastair Campbell's *Contact*[10] review of *Tight Corners in Pastoral Counselling*.[11] Writing as an academic, Campbell found much of the discussion of this 'primal experience' to be 'epistemologically confused and of dubious theological relevance'. The epistemological confusion was related to how, prior to full cerebral development, the foetus could 'know' what was happening to the mother around the time of conception. These claims were based upon pure fantasy, in the strict (and positive) sense of that word. The review reached Frank during his final illness and his last supreme effort was to respond to what he perceived as a threat to the foundations of his work but, sadly, in a way which could see only the negative aspects of the criticism and not the very real tribute to his stature contained within it.

Latterly, Frank's chosen therapeutic response to the mental pain caused by early bad experiences (whether pre- or post-natal) was the method of Primal Integration or the Healing of the Memories. This is essentially a means of helping sufferers relive these earliest bad experiences within a supportive environment. While there are many who will testify to having benefited from this approach, it is evident from a reading of the case histories recorded in John Peters's biography of Frank,[12] that the technique should only be carried out by competent practitioners, and only then under supervision, with provision made for adequate supportive follow-up.

Frank Lake's contribution to pastoral care and education in Britain has been immense. He was a pioneer who launched out into uncharted territory. Many of the ideas which he championed in his early work, particularly the relevance of Object-Relations theory for pastoral care, are now widely accepted. Only the passage of time will reveal the extent to which his later work on the significance of the earliest period of life in the womb is accepted. Interestingly, two new journals[13] have recently appeared devoted to the study of prenatal and perinatal psychology. Perhaps new research will enable a proper evaluation of Frank's contribution in this whole area.

DAVID LYALL
Department of Christian Ethics and Practical Theology,
University of Edinburgh

1

Clinical Theology

WHAT IT IS AND WHERE IT CAME FROM

In the preface to his comprehensive textbook, *Clinical Theology*,[1] Doctor Frank Lake (FL), a medical doctor, psychiatrist and profoundly committed student of the Christian faith, defined the term 'clinical theology' as:

... substantively theology, putting faith, ultimately, not in human wisdom but in the love and power of God, yet meticulously observant of the sound practice of psychiatry and psychotherapy, with the restraints upon religious (or anti-religious) influencing which are properly implicit in them.

He described the book itself in this way:

... a record of my own education as a psychiatrist with a particular concern to help Christian people towards the fullest use of their faith, as a resource, in the treatment of personality disorders and in the whole range of conditions which claim the attention of psychological medicine.

His first chapter defines it more fully:[2]

This whole discipline of Clinical Theology depends on the truth of the Christian claim that in fellowship with God, through Christ and his Church, there are available personal resources which transform relationships and personality. We claim that there is, here, an inflow of being and well-being. In terms of these abstract words which have half lost their meaning, 'the fruit of the Spirit is love, joy, and peace' ... Psychoneurotic persons need these resources above all others. They cannot love maturely, they are prone to gloom, and they are anxious. If love, joy and peace are anywhere available, this diet will cure them.

1

St Paul constantly reminded the Churches he served that these resources are now available.

> Although he was by training a scientist and well aware that his entire teaching hung upon the fine thread of faith, he had become convinced that the 'sound practice of psychiatry and psychotherapy' fell short of offering the kind of help many sufferers needed. At the very end of his book, when discussing some of the most rigid and unyielding types of character defences, he writes:

Those of us who are familiar with the resources available in psychiatry for this whole group of conditions associated with ontological weakness and persecutory states of mind are ready to recognize that they are far from adequate, never fundamentally curative, and inefficient as palliatives. Those of us who have worked for some years in clinical theology have become even more aware of our own utter helplessness in the face of these conditions. At the same time, we have learnt by experience that when faith in Christ Jesus animates the sufferer, it is invariably possible to arrive at a state of creative tension in which the Law of the Spirit of Life in Christ Jesus begins to oppose the 'law of the mind', 'the law of the members', the law of psychological conditioning which constitutes the neurosis . . .

. . . to effect these changes of personality in depth, Christ must be present in power in his Church, in the pastor and in the patient. We cannot use God to alleviate symptoms in self-centred people to the credit of a self-centred Church and a professionally ambitious pastor. Christ works only in those and through those whose desire is to be made 'every whit whole' . . .

> He insisted that the extreme difficulties to be found in ministering to people so afflicted

. . . must not be made an excuse in the Church for passing the buck to the doctors. The Lord Jesus promised rest and refreshment to the weary and heavy laden. He gave, for all time, spiritual food and drink to banish hunger and thirst. In him, the persecuted are to be happy, the spiritually impoverished are to be happy, the hungry-for-right-relationships are to be happy. The loveless are to be given the joy of living in love again, the outcast and the harlot are welcomed into the fellowship of the divine family. All these things Christ offered and much more. If

2

the Church cannot now communicate what her Lord still offers, she should tread more humbly in claiming to represent him.[3]

Fifteen years later, a reviewer in the *Church Times* described the book as having caused 'something of a revolution in the Church's approach to pastoral care', and added: 'Like *Das Kapital, Clinical Theology* is a book which has influenced many, though it may have been read by only a few.' Following its publication, FL discussed his ideas with theologian Don Cupitt and psychiatrist Charles Rycroft in an interview on the Third Programme of the BBC:[4]

Clinical Theology arose out of my concern as a doctor who had worked first of all in India as a parasitologist, and then came to England and changed over into psychiatry, to have something relevant to say to men and women who came to me because I was a Christian and they were Christians. Naturally, at first, I used all the ordinary resources of psychological medicine – drugs, physical treatment, group therapy, hospital work and so on – but then there were some for whom our psychiatric resources just ran out. They had to bear affliction and go on bearing it. The question was this: was there any helpful meaning or resource of meaning that I could offer them in this circumstance? And out of this thought arose what we call Clinical Theology.

Asked whether Christian psychotherapy is superior to secular psychotherapy, or adds anything to it, he responded:

. . . I assure you that the action of the peace of God, if it comes into anybody, does affect their autonomics . . . If this Christian psychotherapy has any resources which are not common to secular psychotherapy, it is the awareness that in the very structure of things, as we believe, God, who made a world which has got into a mess, if you like, at least . . . shows signs of being able to enter into it and share it. So that I think that we can perhaps . . . in dread and in the abyss,[5] be somewhat less afraid, if we or our patients are dragged into it, than secular psychotherapy which, by and large, does admit that where ego defect is very great, or where the death wish is too profound, you had better call off analytic therapy.

Six years later, he was still defending the chosen name:[6]

We have, from time to time, felt that our Association saddled itself with an unfortunate name, since neither 'Clinical' nor 'Theology' are terms which evoke a favourable popular image. We could have changed our name, but have preferred to stand by it, as properly defined.

'Clinical' is precisely definitive of our purpose and training method so long as 'clinic' is defined (as it is in Webster's *Third New International Dictionary*) as: 'A class, session or group meeting devoted to the presentation, analysis and treatment or solution of actual cases and concrete problems in some special field or discipline.'

'Theology' is the substantive term in our title. Our intention in using it is towards the permeating of all relationships with genuine, respectful, wise and costly loving, since this is what God's Word, the *theo-logos* in Christ, is about ... Respect for religious heritages other than the Christian is implicit in this attitude. We regard the joint search of the helper and the person being helped for firmer and deeper resources within the framework of the counsellee's own beliefs to be one of the important functions of counselling.

FL set up his first seminars for training clergy in 1958, but much persuasion was needed before many people in the Church could accept that psychological as well as spiritual insights had a part to play in pastoral care. Christians seemed much quicker to admit failure and uncertainty in others than in themselves. In a Newsletter sent out in 1964 he wrote:

The classical directors of souls have pointed out that if spiritual malaise is not promptly dealt with pastorally, or is mishandled by unwise direction, further disorders will follow which are indistinguishable from the ordinary kinds of 'nervous breakdown'. Christians nowadays, even the clergy, tend to wait until this second phase has been reached before they seek help, so that we, who are psychiatrists, are asked to treat as an 'illness' what was originally, and still remains, a basic disrelationship with God and man. We come into the picture when a chronic lack of interpersonal (that is to say, spiritual) resources has brought relationships in general to an impasse. This, in turn, has produced a regression and the emergence of the bad, fallen relationships of the foundation years. If man's nature has to be cured by the Holy Spirit of its basic distortions of the face of God, then these injured parts are bound to be uncovered and removed. A unified body of medically and pastorally qualified physicians of souls is called for, if we are to understand and deal with complex conditions of this sort, which are common enough among us.

HOW CLINICAL THEOLOGY DEVELOPED

At the Clinical Theology Centre in Nottingham, set up in 1962 when the Clinical Theology Association was founded, FL gathered round him just such a team of 'medically and pastorally qualified physicians of souls' to offer care to the many people, principally clergy, who sought their help. Together, they were also training clergy in an increasing number of seminars around the country. Probably no clearer description of the work and its purpose, and the content of seminars at that time, can be found than in the account given, in 1965, by one of that team, the Revd Michael Hare Duke, in an article for *New Society* called 'Casework theology'.[7] The subheading tells us: 'The clergy today are often caseworkers. A pioneering centre in Nottingham is trying to give them psychological insight into this role – and into the position of the Church today.' (At this time, only male clergymen were conceived of as filling this role. Yet, within a year or two deaconesses, women doctors, social workers, teachers and clergy wives were bringing valuable insights into the seminars.)

Eighteen thousand clergymen of the Church of England deployed in 11,000 parishes cover the total area of this country. The majority of people still turn to the Church at the crucial moments of birth, marriage and death and the parish priest continues to be thought of as someone to take one's troubles to. In addition, through Church schools, as well as by voluntary work among children and youth, the Church is involved with the development of personality. It sets out to answer the most fundamental questions about meaning and purpose, about guilt and reconciliation, which figure so largely in the emotional problems which people present.

At the same time, the clergy are at work in a society which is becoming increasingly aware of the need for effective social work to be done in the community. Very often they feel that they are in a position to undertake a considerable proportion of it. The parson is someone already known, identified with the life of a neighbourhood and yet able to appreciate the wider issues against which a particular need must be understood. Yet often the offers of help by the clergy are discounted by the professional caseworker.

The popular image of the parson swings between the sentimental idealist and the repressive moralist. Clearly neither of these should be allowed to interfere with the delicate problems of a casework relationship. Yet if any individual priest establishes himself with the social services in the area, he is welcomed as a powerful ally ... Since 1958 there has been under way a programme of training designed to help the clergy in their pastoral work and to relate the insights of dynamic psychology to the older language of theology. Those concerned with this experiment have taken the name of The Clinical Theology Association. The purpose of such a title is to emphasize that there is no sense in which the clergy are being trained as amateur psychiatrists. The aim is rather to take the concepts of theology, with which they have traditionally worked, and to give them meaning in terms which seem to be proving their worth in clinical practice ...

The course was offered in the first instance to clergy of the Church of England but, after the first beginnings, doctors and caseworkers joined the Anglicans and Free Church ministers. Three thousand clergy have now taken part in the training scheme.[8]

The method of instruction has been in small seminars meeting for three hours twelve times a year. The syllabus begins with a description of the development of personality through the early years. A particular stress is laid upon the interpersonal aspects, since this is the field in which the parson can be of assistance therapeutically. The depressive, hysterical, schizoid and paranoid personality patterns are discussed. The course aims to teach what the underlying repressed components are and to see how the pastor can make contact with the inner truth of a person ...

The basic assumption of the course is that the person is already at work in this field. He will be seeing people with marriage problems, he will be talking out the personality problems of young people or their difficulties in relationships at work. The training is designed to teach him to listen effectively so that he is not left mouthing irrelevancies or offering advice which only increases the parishioners' guilt by being unacceptable.

These studies move in the second year from the counselling of the individual parishioner to teaching about the various group situations in which the parson finds himself. In work among young people, in marriage preparation, and in the traditional small group meetings of Church life, he will be helped by an understanding of the hidden anxieties of the members. Experiments are encouraged in order to discover whether in such meetings the Church members cannot move towards greater emotional honesty.

The work was originally undertaken by one psychiatrist. The staff of the association has now grown to three doctors and two priests working as pastoral consultants. They have the assistance of a team of voluntary lecturers.

The membership, manner of presentation, and some of the content of the seminars have changed over the years, as attitudes to counselling and being counselled certainly have, but the purpose of the seminars – to make Christian people more effective in caring for others – has not. As we move into the nineties, the tutors (as they are now called) are drawn from clergy and laity, male and female, but are still volunteers. And the crux of the matter is as it was then. (But for 'priest', 'parson', 'parishioner', read 'helper' and 'person seeking help'.) The article continued:

As soon as a priest begins to consider the problems of unconscious motivation, he is bound to look at his own patterns of behaviour. The result of the seminars therefore has not only been in the understanding of his parishioners. The parson has had to face uncomfortable questions about the underlying reasons for some of his theological positions. Sometimes he has had to admit that what he called the will of God was simply a neurotic compulsion to win golden opinions in the parish. The most cherished theory of the priesthood can turn out to be a device designed for keeping people at bay!

. . . Attendance at the seminars has therefore meant for many priests an insight into their own dynamics as well as those of their parishioners. Sometimes they have sought personal help for themselves or their families. From this, as from other referrals, the Clinical Theology Centre . . . has built up an extensive practice both of psychotherapy by the doctors and counselling by the priests on the staff.

The second half of the course – emphasizing group work – has also shown results. From it the priest can gain a new confidence in that traditional tool of his trade: the Christian

7

congregation. The Church's original terms of reference include the ideas of love and acceptance, yet it has often become a club for the like-minded, morally respectable members of society, justifiably attracting to itself the accusation of hypocrisy. By contrast, a therapeutic group in a mental hospital could often give a Christian congregation some salutary lessons in sensitivity to others' needs and tolerance of their badness.

Faced with this comparison, the priest is bound to ask what are the obstacles among the faithful to the expression of the truth which they profess. Why does the Church teach the right things and do the wrong ones? An older generation would have answered in terms of sin. On occasions that category must be still meaningful, but the social sciences have helped to sharpen our observation of what is happening. The behaviour of any group, sacred or secular, can be analysed in terms of its unconscious as well as conscious motivations. When we have seen the insecurities and defensive projections which bedevil any meetings, even the highest councils of the Church, it seems that we have got a good experimental understanding of the self-centredness which is the continual enemy of the Christian gospel.

As a group becomes able to acknowledge its own inadequacies, it is freed from the necessity of projecting them into others and therefore could be ready to be used as a source of reconciliation to a wider circle. Admittedly, the group which has found a sense of security within its membership is notorious for becoming exclusive and a prey to the sect mentality, but a priest who is aware of the natural history of group processes can be on his guard against this . . .

If theology is capable of sustaining its part in this dialogue [*with the social sciences*], it has much to contribute to the healing of society. It can give a sense of meaning and purpose which does not emerge from a clinical examination of the human situation. If, however, it cannot do this, then the parson seems to be faced with the choice of withdrawing into the role of the magician or coming clear from his dogma and joining the case-workers. The Clinical Theology course is a way forward between these two extremes.

THE DISTINCTION BETWEEN A PASTORAL AND A CLINICAL THEOLOGY

Those who took up the challenge to engage in the healing of society found inspiration in the flow of insights which FL provided, helping them to link faith with understanding. The following passage, a continuation of the 1964 Newsletter quoted above, wrestles with the distinction between a pastoral theology for the healthy and a clinical theology for those whose sufferings have damaged their capacity to respond in their usual way:

The pastoral theology which deals with health, rather than with clinical situations, works with whatever human faculties are strong in a person. The sound human capacities of intelligence, reason, imagination, feeling, and the will are actively engaged and stimulated. A clinical theology, however, must come into its own when these desirable human capacities of heart and mind, soul and strength, with which we are ordinarily commanded to love God, can no longer, because of weakness or disease, function as they did in health. God's ability to give us his own life does not, in the last resort, depend upon the will of man at all. His will, unaided by ours, brings us to new birth in places as dark and hidden as the womb itself . . . [9]

Our natural faculties can prepare themselves for the time when they are to be superseded by the energies of God, working in us yet out of our own reach. God himself offers to enter our thinking, feeling and willing, so that they become his. In what state ought a man to be for this change to take place? Does this happen when our human faculties, having exercised and stretched their powers to their fullest extent, hand over the flaming torch of a splendidly functioning humanity into the hand of God? Or does he enter our lives with equal facility when we have, for whatever reason, failed to use our human faculties well or wisely, or when we are so poorly endowed anyway that our contemptible patch of humanity has hardly seemed worth cultivating at all? Does he enter when disease of the body or of the mind has deprived us of all vigour?

When we have neither the strength nor the courage to open the doors of our hearts to let him in, can he enter, as on the evening of the first Easter, 'behind closed doors'? If the weight of lifelong mental pain has crushed the urge to live on, so that the very thought of survival is dreadful and the will longs only for death, can God save us by his own will, without the assistance of any 'acts of will' on our part, such as religion usually demands? Is it sufficient that we simply 'let' him do what he has done for us, and be thankful?

. . . In truth, has he not done all this by his external election of us, before ever we existed to have a will, whether strong in faith or weak? It is for these times of entire lack of confidence in ourselves, or in anything we can do, that Paul's teaching about our election by God from eternity, through time, and back to eternity, is staple diet. This puts our obsessive self-concern to silence. We are simply in his hands. Our final anxieties are his concern. To insist that they remain ours is to wish trouble upon our own heads. Yet to believe this, when the mind is overwhelmed by unidentifiable terrors, or pressed down by despair, is foreign to common sense.

Faith in God is most truly itself when it is no longer dependent on the co-operation of our ordinary faculties. These capacities for ongoing trust, courage and resilience, all of which contribute to the fact that some degree of faith is a common determinant of the secular human spirit, are all too vulnerable. Early deprivation of human care shatters them, perhaps irreparably . . .

Clinical Theology seminars used sometimes to be introduced by a role-play parodying a church warden trying to describe to his vicar his sense of hopelessness and loss of faith. He is strenuously exhorted to Buck Up and Fight the Good Fight by a pastor clearly alarmed by any expressions of weakness or signs of depression from a member of his flock. In his church, all negative feelings had to be fiercely censored. In contrast, FL's article continues:

A clinical theology prepares men to use mental misfortune like a friend, as an unexpected 'negative way' to God, which, doubling back on the usual affirmative route, still meets God in the end, and in much greater depth. It prepares us to do without all kinds of reassurances we commonly demand. The clergyman who wants to be able to 'say something helpful' in order to produce the same tranquillizing effect as the doctor's new medicines (which claim to abolish anxiety) is ultimately looking in the wrong direction. Meditations which induce a peaceful frame of mind are to be compared with pre-medication. They are not the cure. They merely help the patient to prepare to endure an operation for which no total anaesthesia is possible.

We also misconceive the task of clinical pastoral care if we imagine that the main obstacle to our successful conduct of it is that we have not been sufficiently trained to understand the intricacies of interpersonal and intrapsychic conflict. There is a little truth in that. But the lack is not remedied simply by acquiring more detailed knowledge. The essential problem lies deeper than its intellectual interpretation. It is, as we say, existential. It has to do with the wordless agonies of the lonely heart and the wordless healing of grief when it is shared with a friend, in silence. The 'knowing how' of clinical pastoral care is, in the end, obstructed *not so much by our inability to learn* complex facts about human nature *as by our inability to suffer* the painful silences, the anxious involvements, and the reverberation of buried negativities and helplessness in ourselves.

Preliminary instruction for clinical pastoral care depends on an affirmative theology, which demonstrates this or that about God and man with ever-increasing clarity . . . But the work itself will go ahead in the parishes only in so far as clergy and doctors, case-workers and laity, are prepared to experience for themselves the creative darkness, which we are liable to enter when we have been given the courage to abandon our defences. When we write about this, our theology is still affirmative, but it cannot be appropriated until we have ceased to affirm the adequacy of our human capacities in knowing God, until all our highest faculties have been put to silence, and God alone does his eternal work in us.

> The realization that not learned words but a silent sharing of the 'creative darkness' within another human soul might be the kind of help required of them – identification not with Godlike omnipotence but with Christlike weakness – had the paradoxical effect of making pastors who could stand the strain bolder than they had previously been at listening to expressions of private pain. Though at considerable emotional cost, they were freed of the obligation to provide answers to every problem:

Many of the clergy who have studied with us write most encouragingly of the enrichment of their pastoral work. There are critical human situations which formerly they avoided anxiously, which now they accept with something like eagerness. Personality problems and disorders of the human spirit which they would have regarded as beyond the scope of pastoral care are now seen to be directly related to the resources which are ours in Christ. Effective pastoral intervention does not usually bring immediate 'cure' in the medical sense that the disease and its symptoms are miraculously removed. The leopard skin of personality does not change its spots overnight. Particularly with those who have asked for pastoral care only after many months of psychiatric treatment, the nature of the help God gives through his Church is to make what cannot be removed splendidly bearable. Paul's thorn of weakness in the flesh remained. Resting in the power of God, he could glory in this infirmity. Weakness he could use, positively.

The natural man in us tends to reject the paradox that mental pain and spiritual joy can exist together in us, without diminishing either the agony of the one or the glory of the other. The whole personality may be afflicted by a sense of weakness, emptiness and pointlessness without diminishing in the least our spiritual power and effectiveness. This is possible because Christ is alive to re-enact the mystery of his suffering and glory in us. So far as our own subjective feelings are concerned, any inner-directed questioning of our basic human state may produce the same dismal answer as before: the cupboard is bare. While we regard our humanity as a container which ought to have something in it when we look inside, we miss the whole point of the paradox. We are not meant to be self-contained, but channels of the life and energies of God himself. From this point of view our wisdom is to let the bottom be knocked out of our humanity, which will ruin it as a container at the same time as it turns it into a perfect channel . . .

If we are called upon to give pastoral care to the 'sons of want', we must restrain our own ebullience, supposing that we have any. The mode of our activity is now to be as Christ was in his self-emptying. This is meekness: an unlimited power of being held in such restraint that it can be mistaken for weakness, which has no well-being at all. Christ, who was crucified through weakness, became, by that act of obedience, a source of unlimited strength to all those whose lives are hid in his. This hiddenness is essential to the paradox.

Clinical pastoral care must discriminate rightly between the hiddenness which is defensive and sterile, and that which is, in a hidden intimacy, open towards God, so as to be united with his transforming energies in the mystery of the Body of Christ. It requires more than infinite tact, it requires a hidden identification with man's inner wretchedness of spirit, if we are ever to make contact with it.

So it is that much of what we do, when we are sitting with a man who is struggling not to hide himself any longer, is itself hidden in wordless prayer for him. That pastoral care is being given to troubled people cannot, in the long run, be hidden. But the intention of those who engage in it must be to be better known to God than to men.

All this was summed up in one of the early training pamphlets:[10]

The resources being offered are not only the resources of a human relationship, because every man must realize that he can empathize only to a limited extent with the sufferings of others. It is Christ alone who can reach down to the depths of suffering that are before us, and it is of him, and not of ourselves, that we speak. In no sense are we directive as to the manner of life which we think the patient ought to have led, or should lead in the future. Our concern is only to offer him, in the name of the Lord whom we serve, a direct relationship to him, the result of which we confidently know will be a renewal of life. He too will be raised from the death of the spirit, from guilt and from unbelief, into an abundant relationship with the Life-Giver himself, and the personal gifts which his indwelling brings, his love, his joy and his peace.

I have never felt in the least able to systematize this part of the clinical theological interview. It is our business at this moment to be entirely attentive to the Holy Spirit, who will give us, out of all the many resources that Christ's redemptive work has made available, those which we should lay before the troubled person. However much time you have spent on the structure, planning, content and delivery of a sermon, there comes a time when you must leave all these things behind and depend in a direct fashion upon the Holy Spirit. It is precisely so here. With no two people will the approach be identical. This is entirely the Holy Spirit's work, because it is he whose task it is to apply the saving work of Christ to human beings. Yet, because he has called us to be fellow labourers with him, nothing of the care we have taken in listening to the woes and trials of the natural spirit will be lost. It is our share of the burden-bearing.

WHAT WAS NEW ABOUT CLINICAL THEOLOGY?

FL was a great absorber of ideas, reading widely and ever-willing to consider new theories and to experiment with different therapeutic approaches. That his own training in psychiatry encouraged this kind of openness is apparent from this account.[11]

I count myself fortunate in the hospitals in which I trained. I spent a year at 'The Lawn' in Lincoln, under Dr John Goodlad, and then six years at Scalebor Park Hospital in Yorkshire, under the wise and compassionate eye of Dr James Valentine. Both these hospitals, being relatively small and well-staffed, attracted professional people from their localities. A psychotherapeutic approach on the widest possible basis was expected, and there was time to devote to extended investigations. The course for the Diploma in Psychological Medicine at the University of Leeds has also gained a reputation, uncommon in English schools of psychiatry, for a dynamic approach on eclectic lines. The Regional Hospital Board had appointed Dr R. E. E. Markillie as Consultant Psychotherapist, which brought a well-judged Kleinian flavour to our discussions and to the supervision of our cases. But, lest any of my teachers should be embarrassed by this eventual product, I ought to say that the fundamental positions upon which the psychodynamic structure of clinical theology is based, were taught to me, not by any professional teacher, but by my patients.

> He acknowledged a debt to Melanie Klein, Winnicott and Harry Stack Sullivan; to the writings of Fairbairn, Guntrip and Laing for bringing 'the schizoid position into sharper focus', and to Otto Rank, whose 'postulation of birth trauma as the first significant source of personality' he found confirmed in his own practice, especially during the period when he was using LSD–25 as an abreactive agent. At the time his book was published, this notion was less easily accepted, either by doctors or laymen, than it is now.
>
> Since FL's use of LSD in therapy has sometimes raised eyebrows, it may be as well to insert his own statement of why and how he used it before going further:[12]

LSD–25, or lysergic acid diethylamide tartrate, is a mescaline-like drug whose effects were discovered by accident in Switzerland. Apart from some physiological changes in perception which result in hallucinations, of lovely designs, shapes and colours, the main effect of LSD is to lift the areas of repression which cover infantile memories. This effect occurs most favourably where the subject is a patient in need of treatment and already within a good relationship with a therapist.

A minute dose of this medicine is drunk in plain water and after about half an hour its effects begin to be manifest. The ordinary world appears to be seen in an unreal way and the deeper world of past emotions begins to come to the surface of consciousness. It is impossible to forecast which memories will appear first. Sometimes they are extremely happy memories of infancy and the blessedness of life in the first year. On other occasions patients begin to giggle, but the character of the laughter may change into something more hysterical and frightened. This is likely to herald the emergence of the memory of some infantile emotional anguish, usually of separation from the mother within the first nine months of life.

At other times the grown person, even if by now at the age of 50, may relive vividly the anger with which weaning came as an unacceptable experience. The patient under LSD is quite convinced of the reality of these experiences, which are reported often with detail which the patient had no later means of knowing but which can be confirmed from independent observers who were adult at the time.

It is also characteristic that the patient remembers the way in which he reacted to this early emotional stress. The interesting fact is that throughout the rest of life he has tended to react to emotional stress in the same way, that is, for example, by an hysterical clamouring for attention, or a 'schizoid' detachment from relationships which have become too painful to bear, or a depressive defence, whereby the infantile anger is controlled inwardly so that it does not manifest itself. We see here the roots of the psychoneuroses of adult life developing surely and permanently from events in the first year.

One characteristic which seems of major importance is this: many of the most severe sufferers from infantile deprivation within the first six months of life are quite certain that though they were lying in dread and panic because the mother was not there, they made no outward cry of pain or anguish by which the average mother could know that her child needed her desperately. These people were often regarded as unusually good babies because they never cried, and could be left for long periods unattended. If the baby shows an unnatural independence of maternal attention it is doubtful whether this should be matter for maternal congratulation.

One thing is certain, the human infant in the first nine months after birth is incapable of conceiving of itself as existing for very long without the visible presence of its mother. To leave any child too long without attention, or in the dark without company, can lead to severe emotional shocks which give rise later to the psychoneuroses, which manifest themselves in anxiety, phobias, emotional disabilities, depressions, persecutory delusions and the like.

Since the patient is under LSD for about four hours and needs the presence of some understanding person all the time, preferably the therapist, its use is very rare in the busy mental hospitals. On the other hand, analysts have not taken it up as yet, since their often rigid orthodoxy demands a much slower approach, lasting many years to reach the same experience. Even then, in orthodox analysis, the infantile experiences are dealt with by transference, whereas with LSD the recall of the memory is direct and needs very little, if any, interpretation from the therapist.

The model

What distinguished Clinical Theology from other forms of pastoral psychology, and made it particularly attractive to Christians, was FL's explicit assertion that Jesus Christ was the truly normal – though of course in no way average – man. This choice of model for a well-functioning personality, God's 'demonstration Man', is crucial. FL explained it fully in his book, but, writing in the journal *Contact*,[13] Peter van de Kasteele, executive director of the Clinical Theology Association, tells how it came about:

Frank had been working as a medical missionary in India, and then came home to study for his D.P.M. The hospital at which he trained admitted significant numbers of professional people as patients, including clergy and doctors. Frank was alerted to such people, who seemed to be largely ignorant of how to help themselves and how to help others who suffered emotional disturbances and psychiatric illness. He shared his concern with the then Bishop of Bradford, Donald Coggan, that clergy needed further pastoral training to help them listen empathetically and to understand, instead of being afraid and tending to dismiss such suffering when they met it . . .

In the prompt manner which I feel to be characteristic of him, and with much prayer and consulting other people who might be similarly concerned, Frank responded to the Bishop's invitation to provide this sort of training himself. In the autumn of 1958, the first inter-disciplinary seminar was held in Nottingham. Before long, Frank was being invited by other dioceses to explain what he was doing. He travelled long distances to lead seminars, while also practising as a psychotherapist from his home.

A combination of Frank's rather authoritarian Christian upbringing and the pressure of what he was hearing in many hours alongside his psychiatric patients, led him to look for a normative criterion for human personality and interpersonal relationships. 'There are only two alternatives open to model-makers in the field of human personality. Either one proceeds from an examination of human beings as they are, to infer, and later affirm, that such and such a pattern is normal, or one must, as an act of faith, set up a certain pattern as normal, and proceed to examine existing human specimens in the light of it.'[14]

The . . . clinical theological model is founded on the conviction that our Lord's humanity is, and remains, normative.

An informal account in FL's own words is to be found in tapescripts of seminars he conducted for the Post Green Community in Dorset in 1981, the year before his death:[15]

This model actually arose when I was still at Vellore, through having days of discussion with a Swiss theologian, Emil Brunner . . . And he said to me, 'You will find the model that you are looking for somewhere in the life of Christ. I can't tell you where exactly, but I suggest you read John's Gospel, time and again, and I think you will find those qualities in the life of Christ which are the norm for humanity.'

The trouble with Freud and Jung and Adler was that they were all basing a normal psychology on abnormal situations. They were studying the sick, and then they were saying that health is an absence of sickness. Not a positive thing . . .

So that I was driven very early on to say, 'Well, look, what Christian norm can we offer?' And it did seem that even when the critical theologians had done with Christ in the Gospels, certainly he remained the man who prayed, which is not an activity that the natural man feels to be a particularly interesting and sensible thing to be doing. And yet Christ daily has this sense of being, as it were, abiding in the vine – that's a metaphor he continually used himself – that his roots are in the Father . . . that he abides in the Father. And the Father's life is given to him without measure. All this wisdom and love and power, knowledge of God, flows into him, and he gives it out to others.

But then, regularly, he experiences this coming back to the place of dependence on God in prayer, and always his prayer is totally full of trust. The Father's voice is heard: 'This is my beloved Son, in whom I am well pleased.' And all the time this dynamic cycle is fulfilled in the life of Christ . . .

Challenged back in 1966 by Don Cupitt[16] as to how we could know enough about Jesus to posit him as the human norm, given the scant biographical information we have, FL replied:

If you recollect, I don't in any extensive detail go into, or attempt to psychologize our Lord. My basic use of Christ is to say that he is the man who prays, that he is therefore somebody for whom, every day, the sources of being and well-being are outside himself in a relationship with his Father, and that he moves into this relationship with his Father and, in union with him, is loved by God. And then he can say: 'As my Father has loved me, so I love you' . . . but I agree with you that there are many points in my use of this which ought further to be questioned.

He did not, however – even in his last years, when he had come to believe that many of the sources of mental pain lay as far back as in the womb – meet sufficiently convincing arguments to cause him to abandon his model. Shortly before he died he wrote:[17]

Raising the issue of truthfulness means that we cannot escape facing up to the basic disclosure of revelation, that for Christians Christ is the only adequate model for our humanity. He, and he alone, is what human beings are meant to be. If we want to know how our humanity is meant to work, which means the only way it *will* work, we must look more closely at Christ. The Scripture sets him forth clearly as the norm, the model. He is the Way, and insofar as we diverge from him, we have 'gone out of the way' and are lost to the truth of our nature.

Transmarginal stress

What both he and others saw as his own unique contribution to psychiatric thinking was his account of transmarginal stress, his theory that intolerable pressures on an infant, during or soon after birth, could lead to a reversal of its will to live into a desire for death, a descent into the abyss of total despair. He considered it important enough to raise at once, in the radio interview quoted earlier, with Don Cupitt and Charles Rycroft. (As the language is rather specialized, readers unfamiliar with the concept may prefer to return to this passage after reading Chapters 3 and 4.):

. . . I'd like to hear your comment on my use of the Pavlovian[18] concept of transmarginal stress to account for the sharply discontinuous reactions of infancy and later life. You remember that Dr William Sargent, in his provocative book *The Battle for the Mind*, put together the evidence that this transmarginal stress occurs in adults. Subjected to battle horrors or calculated prison tortures, men underwent transmarginal stress into paradoxical reactions. Stimulus and response were inverted. The continuance of painful stress turned the natural struggle to live into the opposite, into a struggle to die . . .

So far as I know, no one has hitherto used Pavlov's concept of transmarginal stress as the main interpretative hypothesis by which to unify those phenomena of discontinuous response conceptually. That is to say, Pavlov has not been used to explain the pathogenesis of withdrawn, schizoid, or autistic personality reactions. Now we have clear evidence that they are brought about by these sudden reversals from the hysterical position of clinging or over-attachment, and are separated from that position by a simultaneous peak of mental pain and a fall into an abyss of dread. Our repeated experiences of sudden, discontinuous reactions of this sort, emerging into consciousness as the traumatic experiences of birth itself, and the first year, are relived under LSD–25, have left us with no alternative but to admit that Pavlov was right when he claimed that psychiatry would not be able to clarify its own subject matter until the supraparadoxical reversals due to transmarginal stress were thoroughly adopted. If the use of this Pavlovian hypothesis is established, it will, I think, be a breakthrough in several directions.

Now, since Dostoievsky, novelists and dramatists have been delineating this abyss and the view of life one gets sitting on the cliff edge either side of it, or existing actually within it. Samuel Beckett, Anouilh, Pinter, Camus, Sartre – and so many others – have been the real specialists on madness and the borderline states. Psychoanalysis has virtually dithered before these horrors, and psychiatry is dedicated largely to the sealing off of these attics and cellars of our mental life with pharmacological glue. Now if Clinical Theology, in so far as it extends the boundaries of psychiatric and pastoral thinking, is validated, it will also extend the ability of the healing professions to empathize with all such venturers into the interior. At times, their nerve fails, but hitherto they've looked for little help from doctors or priests.

There was none. I don't think that any system of clinical pastoral care can match up to today's needs unless it faces squarely these thorny issues for theodicy raised by Job, Pascal, Kierkegaard and Simone Weil.

In the book, I've maintained the view of Fairbairn, Guntrip and others that the ultimate resistance to personality change, and therefore both to psychoanalytic therapy and to pastoral care (if it were to aim again to turn compulsive sinners into good men) – that these derive from a splitting of the self at the very basis of personality. All intractable resistance leads down to this schizoid position of dread in the abyss. It is hardened by the subsequent defensive withdrawal into detachment, introversion, autistic thinking and rigid behavioural patterns, in which anxiety is focused to avoid commitment. Yet, on the other side of the abyss, just before the split actually occurred, anxiety is focused with equal panic intensity on averting separation from the personal sources of being, averting the loss of faith and impending dereliction.

All these repressed defences prevent personality change. The human spirit recoils from the long and bewildering journey back to dependable interpersonal relationships. For, to make this journey, modern man must come down from the ivory towers of self-sufficiency, moving up to a peak commitment panic at the thought of the dark and fearful valley into which it seems he must again descend, and walk for what seems like an eternity of hell (with no certainty of any way out) towards a re-enactment of the primal fall into dereliction and the clinging of separation anxiety.

Now, if all these changes and stages have to be gone through before the human spirit regains the two basic forms of courage – to be embodied as a part of others and, where necessary, to stand alone – then this is a journey few will undertake; nor, in my opinion, can it be undertaken unless the spirit of man is fortified with a power of being greater than his own.

So my last point is to affirm that this is why our whole book is a spelling out, or exegesis, of the Cross of Christ, the extremities of commitment anxiety. We're not able to turn Christ away

from his obedient movement towards Jerusalem and Gethsemane. The baptism of the abyss, the unleashing on him of demonic
forces, the identification with scorn and persecution, rage and
envy, the descent into the hideous valley to taste death for every
man – all these the spirit of Christ encountered and endured.
And then, when help was most needed, in the dark, cold facelessness of dereliction on Golgotha, all the ultimates of separation
anxiety were borne by this Son of God.

At first, Christ seems to bear these things for us. As we obey
him, he protects us against the rigours of this journey. Only later
do we discover that he can bear them in us so that we share
somewhat of the tribulation incident upon change of personality.

So that's why we have called it 'Clinical Theology' . . .

At this point Don Cupitt congratulated him 'on attempting
to plot out connections between modern psychiatry and the
old mystical and ascetical theology', which clearly needed
to be done, but pointed to some of the difficulties implicit
in the attempt. FL replied:

The patient suffering from an anxiety depression doesn't feel 'I
have a bit of experience that is relevant to a psychologist, a bit
more to a psychiatrist, a bit more to a neuro-physiologist, a bit
more to a pharmacologist.' He says, 'I am in a unitary experience
which has many aspects, some of which are philosophical, some
theological, some biochemical.' It's up to us – if we are to meet
people and . . . make sense of what's going on – that we should
ourselves make the effort as helpers to encompass these areas
which are within the patient already unitary.

The discussion ends with him saying:

. . . what we've been trying to do in Clinical Theology is to
suggest that without any distortion of facts on either side [*theological or psychological*], there are such clear and deep correlations
that we ought to bring them back again into pastoral practice . . .
The Church has become so much devoted to positive, definitive,
clarifying theology that it's lacked a theology for these darkness
states . . . if he is there with us, it's about time, I think, that the
Christian clergy and laity began to be able to listen to people
who are in this distress.

Our whole aim in teaching so much clinical psychology is not
to stuff people with ideas that they can talk about to people, but

in order to calm their anxieties so that they can listen and go on listening, and, as it were in the back of their minds, order this turmoil of facts so that they don't pull out of the situation.

2

Mental Health

WHAT CONSTITUTES MENTAL HEALTH?

To be mentally healthy implies that a person has attained to a settled sense of personal identity within his immediate society. He knows who he is among his family and friends, and at work. He can be and do what is expected of him.[1]

> Mental health can be defined in terms of the ideal, from which human beings must, by their nature, fall short. Or it can be defined in terms of what feels healthy in ourselves and looks so in the people we know who are reasonably well adapted to the world as it is. As has been shown, Frank Lake felt that the only adequate model for our humanity must be one that shows us what we are meant to be. And the example he set before us of someone with this 'settled sense of personal identity', who 'knows who he is', is Jesus Christ. In him can be seen personality functioning at its best.
>
> FL returned to this crucial issue again and again in his books,[2] lectures and seminars. In 1978, in response to a request from the magazine *Religion and Society*, he wrote:[3]

It is a moot point whether mental health as the secular psychiatrist in me is implicitly taught to regard it, and mental health as the biblically-based Christian in me receives it, are related as oil is to water, in which case they don't mix, or as healing water to living water, in which case the latter revives the former . . . I fear, but do not avoid, either the radical discontinuity, the 'new mind of Christ' that changes the 'old man's' mind out of recognition, or the manifest empirical continuities in the same human person before and after his *metanoia* or conversion.

. . . There is an implicit definition of mental health in Paul's assurance to Timothy that God's gift through the laying on of hands was 'not a spirit of fear or timidity but the spirit of power and love and of a sound mind' (2 Tim. 1:7). The man in Christ 'has the mind of Christ' (1 Cor. 2:16) and it is 'enough for the disciple to be as his Lord'.

Further on in the article we read:[4]

. . . The pattern of man based on the Son of Man, a pattern which God by the Holy Spirit reproduces in Christians, is in some ways antithetical to the world's notion of what is mentally healthy . . . Its [*the world's*] aims are largely the removal of mental pain from all sources. To such programmes this Man, Jesus Christ, is a disturber of the peace. He introduces new sources of mental pain where before him there was only a dull ache, or the anaesthesia of repression and habit.

Like the good Jews who believed in Jesus (John 8:31), many Christians . . . have hopes of better health by following this Master. He encourages us, as he encouraged them, that if we continue in his word we will not only be his disciples, but live in the truth about ourselves and God. We will be really free.

. . . Christ's model for mental health begins, like the Eucharist, with a collect for purity. Reflecting on the main thrust of this prayer, we could call it the 'collect on honesty'. God is one 'to whom all hearts are open, all desires known, and from whom no secrets are hidden' . . . Frankly, this model terrifies us . . . Our progress towards mental health in the Churches advances step by step with our willingness to be known by our neighbours as that collect says we are known by God . . .

There is not enough space to reproduce here FL's analysis of accepted psychiatric models for mental health, or his reasons for finding them unsatisfactory. These can be found in his books. But he firmly rebuts the suggestion that the average man can be considered 'normal':[5]

[The Christocentric view] is a view of the 'norm' which eschews and recoils from the average man's low view of his life possibilities for growth and betterment. It sets its sights on the Spirit-filled Christ, endowed with charismata for ministry gifts which show God's intention to deal with all those deep resistances to radical change that make the average man so compulsively mediocre. My dentist can say that, for my age, I have an average number of surviving teeth, with an average number of fillings,

24

and we can accept that as the 'norm'. But dental *health* must envisage the possibility of preventing decay. There is no intrinsic reason why I should not have, as some people do have, thirty-two sound teeth at sixty-four years of age. That norm is the optimum . . .

> He acknowledges that the Christian model for mental health presents a difficulty for non-Christians and, in seeking common ground, explores several current definitions, but finds weaknesses in all of them. That of the World Health Organization – 'Health is a state of complete physical, mental and social well-being and not merely the absence of disease and infirmity' – he categorizes as 'ambitious', and even less capable of realization than Christ-based definitions.

. . . Mental health, if it is to mean more than the theologically inept and ultimately meaningless notion of cheerful and brisk adaptation to one of our already discredited Western or Eastern cultural styles, [implies], I think we would agree, that we must explore ultimate meaning and purpose . . .

[But] it would be fatally easy for me to begin here an argument about the ways in which one or another of the major world religions promotes or hinders 'mental health', as though I, being a mental health professional, possessed a yardstick by which to judge among them . . . As psychiatrists, we have established some accumulated facts about mental illnesses and can often alleviate their symptoms. But we are not competent, as a profession, to pontificate about the purposes of human life, even though we would affirm that a sense of meaning and purpose is essential to mental health.

. . . The mental health professional man's training equates the truth of anything with the manner of its presentation, demonstration, and proof by means of the scientific method. The value of this method is the scientist's only ultimate value . . . So that an apparently fundamental question such as, 'Why is there something, not nothing?' is ruled out. It cannot be asked because the method we worship, as other men worship God, cannot either ask or answer it. For a scientist to ask such questions is to become a heretic, worse than a heathen.

The central claim of Christ and of Christians is that those whose faith rests on him, who live by his Word and Person, inherit eternal life. According to his promise, they will be, 'with him, where he is' beyond death. Their adoption, as sons of his Father, is to 'an eternal inheritance'. *If it is true, this is a mental health resource of immense potential.* One could say that its steadying effect through the vicissitudes of life would operate powerfully even though, in the end, the Christian woke up after death to find that he had committed himself to a glorious mistake. Some men's mistakes might be more conducive to true humanness than some other men's time-bound certainties.

The scientifically-controlled experiment required to establish the truth or falsehood of what Christ claims to give to those who place full reliance on his word, can never be set up – not in a way to satisfy scientists, though it might well satisfy a jury. It is Christ who points to the fruits of belief and unbelief: 'By their fruits ye shall know them.' Taste and see. Here is a law of evidence . . . [6]

. . . Whichever way we look at it, in religious or secular terms, the teleological dimensions, the meanings and values around which people organize their lives, are important contributory resources for mental health. We cannot do justice to this subject without taking into consideration all theological convictions and philosophies, all ideologies which have the force of religions, and those cultural institutions, like the joint-family system in India, which still have great force and relevance as part of 'the princi-palities and powers'. These structures, which largely condition our responses, and from which it is never easy to break free, can be decisive positive factors in maintaining mental health, or negative ones in destroying it.[7]

By the early seventies, FL had worked widely with clergy-men of various denominations, seeing them as colleagues, seminar members, tutors-in-training, and as patients in his psychiatric practice. These men had a role to maintain and a heavy investment in appearing to be model family members and in complete control of themselves and their world. This meant living, in many cases, a lie. Frank gave much attention to this problem, for, as he did not shrink from admitting, he shared it. In a lecture given in Edinburgh in 1967, he spoke of himself as:

'. . . a man who cannot give himself in love' and who 'gave it up and decided to barricade himself behind books and write a book so large that it ought to have been sold with wheels attached!'[8] [The unabridged *Clinical Theology* ran to 1282 pages. Ed.]

The following passage comes from the draft of an article provisionally entitled, 'The health of the clergy',[9] which suggests one way of assessing mental health:

A man's health or illness is not an individual matter. Properly speaking, it is the sick or healthy functioning of the interaction between himself and the various areas of life which go to make up his existence.

Can I use a simple model, with four concentric circles? Let the innermost area represent the central selfhood. Its immediate environment is his own intra-psychic world, the world of his own needs, his fantasies, his experiences, stored in conscious and unconscious memory, and all his secret hopes and fears. These needs and expectations may be so overwhelming as to occupy most of his attention. On the other hand, he may have 'a heart at leisure from itself', so as to be free to interact generously and openly with all the outer circles.

In the second circle we put all his most intimate relationships . . . relationships between the man and his wife, with his children, with his own parents, alive or dead, and with all their varied expectations of him, present and past. (If the parents are dead, I suppose, in one sense, you'd have to put them in the innermost circle. But they may act as though they were alive and, in this sense, they exist in both.) I have known men relating strenuously to parental expectations, which represent what the mother or father expected of them twenty or thirty years ago, even when the actual live parent now has no such expectations. For some unmarried clergymen this second circle is almost empty. The tragedy is that there are also some married clergymen for whom the intimate circle is virtually an area of non-interaction. Nothing happens in it.

This is often because he conceives himself only a person relating to the third concentric area, which is the parson in relation to his congregation and their expectations, the Bishop and his fellow clergy and their expectations. The man's identity as a person may be wholly swallowed up by his role as the vicar of a particular parish at a particular time, and all the stylized relationships that the role requires of him.

The fourth concentric circle represents his relationship to society and the community outside his professional life. Some clergymen would deny that this area has any validity for them at all. Others have become so disenchanted with the relationships between themselves and the third circle of parochial life, that all their emotional investment is in some form of activity outside the parish. They feel sterile, if not sterilized, and quite hopeless in regard to the self-to-circle-three interaction. They may take up local or borough politics, chairmanship of the Samaritans, local representation of the N.A.M.H., or some other extra-ecclesial activity within the community, not as an extension of pastoral care of the congregation but as a substitute for it.

He then concludes:

The emotional health of a pastoral person can be regarded as significantly present if he is maintaining an interaction between himself and each of these areas in such a way as is mutually need-fulfilling. He does not neglect either his own inner life of the mind, nor his own wife and children, nor the deepest needs of his congregation, nor their administrative requirements, and he has time and interest available to relate to the community. He may have other responsibilities, such as the training of curates or lay workers, and for these, too, he finds some genuine place in his life.

Can we assert that personal mental and emotional health can be present even though one or more of these areas is neglected or squeezed into insignificance because of exaggerated attention to any one of the others? If we accept this concept, then we must look beyond the clergyman himself and his symptoms before we make any decision as to his real health as a person.

If fewer clergy nowadays seem as drastically cut off from their inner selves as FL found them, some of the credit must be his, though, sadly, his own emotional resistance to involvement in circle two appears to have persisted, in some degree, to the end.[10] However, his call to personal openness was not addressed only to professional people. The following comes from the general article quoted earlier:[11]

... Whereas, on the one hand, Christ attacks the character lie at the heart of human social organization, he is immediately at the side of those who, having been its victims, are breaking free into painful honesty. Not only, in his ministry, does he identify with social outcasts and those for whom religious society can find no place – because they manifest openly what others only practise in fantasy or secretly – Christ identifies with them immediately. So much so that he suffers the same fate at the hands of religious society. This [*painful honesty*] and nothing less . . . must provide our criteria for mental health.

Christ acted in judgement with a firm 'no' to the cultural lie, to the falsehood systematized in religious organizations. He would say 'yes' to those who 'do justice, love mercy, and walk humbly with God' . . .

IMAGES OF GOD

Earlier, FL was quoted as saying (perhaps with tongue in cheek) that faith in God is 'a mental health resource of immense potential' even should that faith eventually prove mistaken! One of his enduring themes was the effect on the personality of the 'gods' forged within each one of us by our earliest, long-forgotten experiences. In 1967, he gave a radio talk on 'Images of God',[12] which starts like this:

For many years I lived in India. The Hindu religion is by far the most accommodating to the variety of man's natural images of God. Hinduism as a whole does not set out to correct these images. No image of god takes absolute precedence over any other. What I find intriguing is that, underneath the crust of cultural conformity and doctrinal orthodoxy, I find, in Christians, all the variety of gods and images of gods encountered in Hinduism.

In the course of an illness, such as a nervous breakdown, in the course of therapy, as the depths are searched, and indeed in the course of healthy spiritual changes of personality, a succession of widely differing images of God will dominate our minds in turn. A depressed Christian may complain in the same interview of an angry god condemning him for an unforgivable sin, and a few sentences later bewail the fact that he cannot believe that god cares anything about him. These two images are incompatible and contradictory. If he turns to Christian faith for an image of god and his attitude to a depressed man, neither of these sick images can stand as true.

I write the word 'god' with a small 'g' except where I refer to the Judaeo-Christian account of God. Then I use the capital 'G'. You may disagree, and insist, as Ludwig Feuerbach would have done, that here, too, I ought to use a small 'g'. The essence

29

of religion, Feuerbach claims, is that it fancies its object and its ideas to be superhuman. That this is an illusion is said to be hidden from the religious.

In more modern, psychoanalytic terms, his counterpart would say that man has projected his own intra-psychic object relations, with mother and father and other big people from his infancy, on to the natural world, as if they were actual, supernatural powers, and that they have got stuck in position like 'gods'. Man cannot withdraw the projected images as he would do if he had insight. He cannot say, with a laugh, 'That's just my mind playing tricks on me.'

You see that I have conceded that many images of god are derived from the earliest period of infancy, particularly the foundation year. I would go further, and say that all the various personality patterns to which names are given by psychiatrists and social workers are each associated, quite specifically, with one or other of the regularly occurring images of god.

I would group two of them together, the depressive and the obsessional, as deriving from readily identifiable images of a god who, in this case, is undoubtedly a dutiful but over-strict parent. These are the images of god that keep an eye on many Anglicans in the congregation at matins. He rules wherever righteousness is felt to be the acquisition of those who work harder than others, of those who keep to the religious conventions . . . who lean over backwards to conceal from this stern, repressive god all resentment and rage, however justified, all doubt of his wisdom, all distrust of his providence, all excursions into the fleshpots of Egypt. Such people conceal everything naughty in themselves while pointing it out in others. This god keeps his subjects in a constant state of guilt, and constantly working to make reparation.

If the god of the obsessional position sits enthroned in the mind alongside the god of the potentially depressed, the demand is even more inflexible and rigid . . . Much religion and much church-going, as well as many aspects of the desire to excel in any walk of life – not least housekeeping – are in part motivated by the . . . edicts of this moralistic god of the depressive position, whether there is a clinical depression present or not.

Match these gods against the image of God in Christ in the New Testament and they collapse. If, says Paul to the Galatians, you try to get right with God by doing what the law commands, you . . . automatically cut yourself off from the power of Christ . . . If you are weary, don't beat yourself up, take a rest, in him. The depressive person standing in front of his image of God does not know where to put his murderous rage. He has contemplated suicide as the only way out. The image of God that he gets from the Cross of Christ is a kind of invitation to vent the rage that threatens to kill him upon God. God can take it. God feeds his murderers on the image of the broken body and the shed blood. The murder is theirs, the love his.

What has happened to us when these rigid, legalistic images of god have come to dominate our thinking and feeling? Briefly, a regression to infancy has taken place. All the problems and predicaments of our earliest years, together with our emotional reactions to the people who surrounded us, or failed us then, become present again in our minds as if they were happening in the present. What puzzles us, and makes the infantile origin of these images and feelings about ourselves and the powers that be so hard to recognize, is the further fact of repression. These infantile images have been hidden away in the back room of our minds since babyhood. We have no ordinary memory of ever having seen them before. These two mechanisms, which are apt to occur when we are under too much stress . . . account for the emergence into the conscious mind of a variety of images of god.

When this occurs, for instance, in the course of a depressive illness, the 'successful' treatment of the condition, whether by anti-depressive medicines, electrical treatment, psychotherapy, or clinical pastoral care, will re-establish repression and reverse the regression, so that we face life again as adults. The infantile image of an unhappy me, dominated by unjust, unhelpful, rage-provoking powers, falls back into limbo. The image of god we had before our illness – which in most Christians is a combination of God images culled from Christ and the New Testament, together with a variety of reactions to god images still concealed, though nonetheless influential – this mixed image is restored to the mind as recovery (if that is the right word for it) takes place . . .

> FL goes on to describe the gods associated with other personality patterns – archaic, enslaving gods that lurk in our unconscious minds. He returned to this theme in one of his Newsletters:[13]

. . . In association with each of the diagnosable patterns of personality disorder there is a regularly occurring, predictable and explicable distortion of the image of God . . . Certain revelation truths about God as Christ reveals him are specific in their opposition to these morbid images . . .

It is the task of the practical theologian, through his 'clinical training', to know how to evoke conscious awareness both of the false images that inhibit faith and of the true images that foster it . . . It has pleased God to reveal his Son *in* us as well as *to* us. If the crucified and risen Christ is revealed *in* a man, the true image in all its paradoxical complexity has been formed in him. The heart's eye has been healed. The vision of God has reconciled the images. Here is a man made whole in love and without fear. I have met such men and women, not often, but enough to recognize the authentic transformation.

THE DYNAMIC CYCLE

FL's Christian model for personality at its healthiest, and the psychodynamic theory of personality formation to which he adhered as a psychiatrist, came together in his formulation of the Dynamic Cycle. We find it pre-figured in an article he wrote in 1952, when he was still a medical missionary:[14]

. . . The love, the life and the light of Christ are all communicated in a true medical mission. But popular clamour would keep us wholly engaged in the healing of the sick. We yield to it at the peril of our spiritual usefulness. We must belong primarily to Christ, and learn from him the path of his priorities amid the maze of useful and beneficent possibilities. This means that two dynamic movements are vital to us: the withdrawal for prayer and the return for guided service.

The Dynamic Cycle has served as the basis for all Clinical Theology training from its earliest days to the present. With its input and output phases, the cycle is analogous to the respiratory and circulatory systems of the body. What is drawn into the heart and lungs is given out to the extremities of the body, only to return to the source for refreshment and renewal so that the cycle can begin again. All this is fully explored in *Clinical Theology*. The following excerpts are taken from one of the training pamphlets:[15]

This model was derived from a study of the adult life of Christ . . . in his relations to God and man. We observe what

32

THE DYNAMIC CYCLE

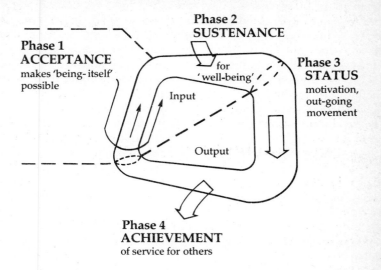

Phase 2
SUSTENANCE

Phase 1
ACCEPTANCE
makes 'being-itself'
possible

for
'well-being'

Phase 3
STATUS
motivation,
out-going
movement

Input

Output

Phase 4
ACHIEVEMENT
of service for others

seems to be a fundamental dynamic inflow and outflow. Christ moves away from attention to human events to attend to his Father and to speak with God . . . This is portrayed as responsive activity, sustained by the Holy Spirit. By it his divine-human existence attains its full essence. *Being* is filled out in becoming *well-being*. He is Son of God and Son of Man, rightly related to the Source Person in both aspects of his being. In this regular mindfulness of his resources of being and well-being, Christ is normative of what man is created and called by God to be.

This Godward movement in the life of Christ is followed by a move towards his human environment. Here, among people, he gives out in service the varied God-given resources of loving, accepting, forgiving, strengthening, healing, feeding, interpreting, promising, of mediating God's action with grace, glory, power, truth and joy, all of which became his through that other life of fellowship with God and intercession for the world.

This twofold movement, away from attention to men to attend to his source in God, and then from total immediate attention to his Father to give full attention to people, seems fundamental to his health and wholeness. He draws attention to his total dependence on and limitation by the Father. His key word is obedience. As he hears, so he speaks. As God acts, so he acts.

This pattern of obedient withdrawal to God as the human being's Source-Person and of subsequent return to people in service does not characterize the 'natural man' among us. We express our own individuality independently and are proud of it. It does, however, characterize what we know about the source of the most healthy human personalities in their early years, in relation first to the mother and then to the father of the child. It also characterizes the dynamics of the therapeutic relationship, whether individual or group. In both these situations, dependency is acknowledged as part of a healthy cycle of interpersonal events . . .

We employ this model to analyse the fundamental mother-baby relationship. We are assured that dependency, *unconditional acceptance* and *sustenance* are vital for the input phases which make for a normal healthy selfhood in infancy . . .

We would expect, for instance, that a 'block' to the mother-baby relationship in Phase 1 of the cycle, where the baby must wait for 'being-itself' through the coming of the mother to attend to it in person, would reduce the power of being-in-relatedness which the infant has retained from previous well-functioning cycles . . . To lose 'being-itself' is an almost irremediable disaster . . . We would predict, therefore, that the most severe personality disorders, most disruptive of healthy selfhood and relationships, would occur as a result of interruption of this first phase of the cycle . . .

We would have to predict that a class of personality disorders exists in which what is diminished or lost is not being-itself (for the source-person is now present, or rememberable), but well-being. The source-person in this case cannot or does not make the experience of 'abiding' for *sustenance* at Phase 2 of the cycle a satisfactory, meaningful and fulfilling experience. The baby is identified, not with gracious mothering, but with loss of rights and humiliation . . . Such persons experience themselves as let down, or weakened. This identity of an unacceptable 'I am not much good', 'I never am, or do, well' feeling, fixated in primal experience, will in many cases arouse a reaction of denial and an attempt to prove the opposite.

Phase 3 implies eventually (though not in earliest infancy) a conscious moving away from the source-person, strong in the sense of *status*, with the identity of one who exists as a whole person. Looking back, there can be a reflective recognition of the way in which one has been loved and brought into being. Looking forward, there is an expectant readiness to enter into a similar quality of trustful and helpful relations with other people. This move . . . implies a readiness on the part of the source-person to permit the necessary degree of separation to occur . . . Smother-love and apron strings frustrate the normal expression of this courage-to-be-as-oneself-alone . . . Should this failure to move in Phase 3 be fixated, troublesome character problems will result . . .

The 'block' may occur at Phase 4 by the denial of the right or possibility of the *achievement* of some work or skill or service that is personally and socially meaningful. This must cause, if it is severe or prolonged, some stunting of character development. This crisis is inherent particularly in later childhood where the attainment of skills and their recognition is the main matter in hand. But at every stage, in every crisis, every transition has its success or failure, and a sense of acknowledged achievement is important . . .

This model is based, in its presentation of 'normal', healthy dynamics on the recorded aspects of the human and Godward relationships of Christ. It takes him to be the pattern for our humanity at its fullest. To value Christ in this way involves and arises out of faith. That God was made man for man is improbable and paradoxical. It cannot be made scientifically probable, much less be open to proof. Its acceptance could never be made inescapable or its rejection illogical . . .

From Christ's adult dynamics . . . we have derived a model for normative relationships, from babyhood through the developmental phases to old age.

What the Dynamic Cycle makes clear – though it is not always apparent to potential counsellors at the outset – is that none of us can give more than we have been given, or help more than we ourselves have been helped, unless we can learn to face and overcome obstacles and resistances deep within ourselves. The ideal pattern for the healthy soul is to grow in loving acceptance and nourishment into a sense of personal value and well-being. Only out of that abundance can we give of ourselves in work and loving relationships and in service to others. But then, when our resources become depleted, we will need renewed access to our source of strength and hope, in God and in our most vital human relationships. Denied that, there will be a

THE DYNAMIC CYCLE IN THE LIFE OF CHRIST

1 ACCEPTANCE
of Christ the Son by his Father; the voice from heaven 'This is my beloved Son in whom I am well pleased.' (Mt 3:17, 17:5)

Christ's response to dependence as a Son and as man, is to pray. (Lk 6:12, 9:18, 9:28)

He faces crucifixion in the garden praying. (Lk 22:44)

He knows that he has constant access. 'I know that thou hearest me always.' (Jn 11:42)

2 SUSTENANCE
Christ abides in the Father. His well-being derives from this. 'The only-begotten Son which is in the bosom of the Father.' (Jn 1:18)

'As the Father has loved me, so I have loved you.' (Jn 15:9)

Christ is given the Holy Spirit and his gifts, all without measure. (Jn 3:34)

'I am in the Father and the Father in me.' (Jn 14:11)

4 ACHIEVEMENT
This is strictly limited to the Father's will. The Son can do nothing of himself but what he sees the Father do. (Jn 5:19, 30, 8:29, 10:36-7)

He can speak nothing of himself but what he hears from the Father. (Jn 8:26, 28, 38)

'The words that I speak unto you, they are spirit, and they are life.' (Jn 6:63, 8:51)

To be the light of the world, so that those who follow him do not walk in darkness. (Jn 8:12, 9:5)

To finish the work of redemption God gave him to do. (Jn 4:34, 17:4, 19:30) 'I must work the works of him who sent me while it is day.' (Jn 9:4)

3 STATUS
'I am from above.' (Jn 8:23)

'I am the Son of God.' (Jn 10:36)

'I am not alone.' (Jn 8:16-18, 29)

'I am the light of the world.' (Jn 8:12, 9:5)

'I am the living bread which came down from heaven.' (Jn 6:51)

Everything is entrusted to him by God. (Mt 11:27)

The Father is glorified in the Son. (Jn 14:13)

Jesus said, 'Hereafter shall ye see the Son of Man sitting on the right hand of power.' (Mt 26:64) diminution in our state of health, probably in accordance with a well-established reaction pattern laid down in infancy.

TRAINING FOR COUNSELLING

In 1967, in a letter to the Bishop of Southwark, FL made a strong case for a positive theological, as well as psychological, underpinning to pastoral counselling:

Pastoral counselling, concerning itself as it does with the ultimate God-given aims and meanings of human life, is one of the few disciplines which cannot properly begin to understand itself at a secular level, and then accept the necessity to import theology as a foreign body at a later stage when all the conceptual framework has been worked out on alien models (based not on Christ but on fallen man). I would attribute many of the difficulties into which clinical pastoral care in the United States of America is running to this setting of the cart before the horse. The very ways we think about and understand clinical pastoral care must derive from Christian involvement and perception of what is involved for people in the strange victory of Christ, for us and in us . . .

Attentive listening to, and total acceptance of, anyone coming to a counsellor for help formed the cornerstone of the Clinical Theology training. This calls for emotional toughness and insight in the counsellor, qualities dependent on the love and nourishment available to them in the input phases of the cycle. But FL's seminal tome had not yet been published when clergymen, not all of them aware of the shortages within themselves, joined the first seminars in the late fifties:[16]

. . . Thousands of the seminar members during the first ten years were clergymen in the traditional mould. They had been drawn to the then-popular image of the pastoral role being augmented by a little training in counselling techniques. They hoped to increase the range of their usefulness to parishioners in distress . . . by the acquisition of some skills. I travelled the length and breadth of the land, and realize, in retrospect, that I learned to recognize a rather sharp distinction, in any group of a dozen parsons (soon with the addition of some Methodist

37

and Free Church ministers), between three or four men who were keen actually to practise counselling, to plunge in and make errors of judgement that revealed skews in their own personalities, and enjoy it hugely, without being in any way threatened, and three-quarters of the group who made it clear that this was not what they had come for.

Not only did I recognize this sharp difference of intention to personal involvement, I made it my business to cater for both categories of learner. With the reluctant, all I could do was model, in my own responses, how I was myself relating to them, patiently hoping that the example of the freer men would . . . encourage them by seeing others do it, without bad effects and with many good ones.

I think I may say that the larger section polarized, between those who began to use the skills sensitively, increasing in empathy, genuineness and respect of the counsellee as a person – not as an object of their skills – and the rest who, sensing that what we called counselling would involve their personalities in commitments which aroused too many anxieties, remained on the fringe until we came to the theory. Here they could excel and argue with the best . . .

> Apart from the increase in lay and female members, the seminars changed over the years. Not in their content (for the Model and Dynamic Cycle held up well to testing and application in diverse pastoral situations) but in the greater emotional involvement of group members. In 1975, FL reported on some of these changes in *Contact*:[17]

. . . The seminar brochure nowadays states quite clearly that their purpose is 'to enable those who work with people to become aware of the resources which can facilitate their growth as persons and helpers.' There are now three elements in each seminar meeting, the first of which is entitled 'Growth group activities', the second, 'Practising effective counselling', and the third 'Relevant knowledge'. Those who are not prepared for this moderate degree of commitment self-select themselves away from the seminars. The level of commitment of those who do join is quite high . . . All the members know that they will practise, in various settings, 'the offering to each other of those attitudes which are known to make for helpful counselling.'

In 1964 I wrote of 100 clergymen in that year who had come to Lingdale for help because of some personal anxiety, depression or other crisis. The swing to drugs diminished this flow. The somatic cry emerging from painful memories is now stifled, not listened to or valued. This is regrettable, since our shared understanding of the psychodynamics of anxiety, depression and the phobias has grown out of all recognition over the past ten years. We can now offer a much better service to those who suffer in these ways than we did then. We are much better grounded in the bodily realities of these states through our assimilation of bioenergetic, gestalt and primal therapy theory and practice.

In those days, we relied, as theologians tend to, on *words* of understanding and interpretative concepts, both from psychotherapy and from the Gospel. Of course, we also dealt with feelings, but the connections we made from feelings to the mind were emphasized, to the neglect of those connections which exist between feelings and the body. We now understand anxiety and depression as whole-person states in which the bodily components tend to be overlooked. This holds up the whole process of therapy, although, once attention is drawn to them, they can change, and the emotional blocks move with them.

We had no conception then of the profound effects of deepened breathing and the ability of fully 'inspired' human beings to reconnect, relive, and reintegrate split-off aspects and experiences of infancy. This breakthrough is crucial, since all our stress syndromes, our neuroses, and personality 'hang-ups' were laid down in this earliest period. The three staff psychiatrists occasionally used LSD to open the gates of memory. Not now. Fresh air, deeply inspired, in a caring group, competently led, by people ready to work at re-owning [*archaic infantile feelings*], does it so much better.

He then rehearsed some of the debates and disagreements that characterized the formative years of the Clinical Theology movement:

This takes me back to the decisive turning point in the life of CTA as an organism. Until 1968–9 the staff included psychiatrists and pastoral consultants who were, for personal and, in the best sense, 'political' reasons, concerned about the 'image' of the Association. We were all uncomfortable about the extent to which the Clinical Theological input was too largely the work of one man, embodied in a tome of fearful size, which had been too much for reviewers to read, let alone understand.

The fact that we had deliberately based our anthropology on

Christology, viewing Christ as the 'normal man', or 'norm' for man's dynamic input-output flow, was unthinkable to theologians sliding towards 'the Death of God' or [to] the American Pastoral Counsellors and Clinical Pastoral Educators still content with a Rogerian anthropology. Allergic to irrelevant, nonemphatic God-Talk (as we also were) had become resistant to and inhibited about spirituality. For our part, a relevant and inductive spirituality was the life-blood of our work.

Clinical Theology has always deliberately based pastoral care on the character of the recipient. Different personality types seem to call forth widely different responses from the counsellor. This, in our view, determined the appropriate style of pastoral activity. It was reported to me that Seward Hiltner was opposed to this characterology, and certainly his colleagues at the Menninger . . . were then inveighing against diagnosis. They saw that 'labelling' could, in psychiatric circles, be a form of 'libelling'. We, too, deplored this tendency, but saw beyond it to a realization that, if diagnostic differences are a way of 'seeing through' into basic points of origin of personality distortion, they are a necessary part of our discipline.

The non-acceptance of this Christocentric characterology and the new styles of pastoral care and theological reflection to which it was giving rise, by the theological faculties on the one hand and by the psychiatric hierarchy on the other, could not fail to be disturbing. For some of the staff and a few of the Council members, this and other factors led to a parting of the ways . . . The clergy tutors, about 80 of them, were fairly solidly for continuing in spite of this failure to convince the establishments. The Bishop of Derby, Cyril Bowles, who had some confidence in the original concept and in our ways of working, became the Chairman and the process of rebuilding began.

The clue to the health of this rebuilding has been the influx of ideas and training opportunities from a succession of leading clinical pastoral educators from the States. The whole tutorial body, including the Staff and the Director, have been students at their feet, learning together and assimilating what we could. We expanded our practice, applying what fitted well with our own style, or in some cases, transformed both our styles and ourselves also.

They are a distinguished group. John Maes, Howard Clinebell, David Switzer, Bill Johnson, Jim Ashbrook, Art Foster, John Patton, Bob Leslie, and Mike Reddy, a Jesuit who, though British, spent six years in the States specializing in Transactional

Analysis. Each of them has introduced us to some new and important resource for the clinical pastoral undertaking . . .

We do not believe that proficiency in any one of these methods is a total or even adequate approach to therapy. We cannot claim to do what they do. We have our own amalgam. At the same time we do not wish to use without acknowledgement the work these innovators have written about so movingly, which we have read so avidly and adopted or adapted with such good effect.

This all seems a long way from where we started in Clinical Theology. In fact, we are now just beginning to arrive at a true word of God for the distresses of our day.

His own amalgam was consistent in refusing to reject either what he had found to be true in the practice of psychiatry or in the practice of his religion, as another excerpt from his 1978 article on mental health shows:[18]

. . . Must we not say that all mental health programmes that propose a new direction for man, with new and life-enhancing possibilities, should be treated with caution? *Caveat emptor*, watch the seller, and take a double good look at his product. Each mental health programme needs to stand up to a double critique, one from a depth psychology that is familiar with primal and perinatal phenomena and the fixations to which they lead. Intra-uterine life, birth, and the immediate postnatal period are rich in sources for transcendental experience, both of heavens to be sought and hells to be avoided.

The other critique derives, for Christians, from the words of Christ. If we wish to be his disciples, he compels us in freedom to centre ourselves upon his word and person as the one reliable road to truth, to freedom, and to our eternal destiny in him . . . It is only as conviction grows that they are the only sane way forward for man that we can attempt to write about theological issues in mental health . . .

If Christ is not who he claims to be in this matter, we are following a liar and an impostor, and are blind leaders of the blind. The faith that, through him, we really can see the truth is a faith statement. It cannot be proved . . . The fact that it inspires such certainty in use that we would rejoice to die for it does not make it true. To live for it is to incur crosses and persecutions. It introduces a dialectic into our discussions of mental health. And I notice that humanists who are brave

41 16977

enough to look at the human condition as one which encloses a vital lie,[19] even in our best and most adequate characters, are offended by the refusal of churchmen to see these things, and not by Christ's relentless pointing them out. The need to stand firm theologically does not put me out of sympathy with my humanistic colleagues in the growth movement.

FL repeats his definition of mental health, in slightly different words, again and again, presumably because most of us are too possessive of our inner secrets to hear it. Here it is once more:[20]

To be mentally healthy is about living in the light of truth and reality. It means being clear and transparent to one another, not opaque or, like guilty Adam, hidden. It is being open to inner illumination or insight, so that we know ourselves down to the depths of our hearts and desire so to be known by others. In this sense, to have a fully healthy mind is to have the mind of Christ. Our faith statements focus on him as the Logos, the Meaning of man for man. He came then, and he comes now, as a Light to shine in the darkness that is in us and around us.

3

The Origins of Mental and Spiritual Anguish

THE WOMB OF THE SPIRIT

Introducing his pamphlet on the origins of personal identity in the late 1960s, Frank Lake wrote:[1]

. . . The very earliest experiences which can lead to disturbed feelings of identity . . . take their origin in the distresses of babyhood. This does not imply that we esteem the individual's current social contingencies and environmental conflicts as of relatively small importance. Quite the contrary. Pastoral care is intimately concerned with present-day issues and it is in this area that the Church, as a community, contributes most to restore to health a damaged sense of identity. But these contemporary issues, though complex, are not likely to be missed in a pastoral interview . . . Nor do they, of themselves, give rise to strange identity feelings such as can defy pastoral understanding, unless the intensity of the present stress has been so severe as to drive the mind into a regression. It is then that the adult 'I' falls back into primitive crises of identity which have all along been preserved unabated in the deep mind. These then emerge in consciousness with all their original concomitants of now inexplicable bodily and mental symptoms.

This is the kind of occasion on which the untrained clergyman seldom sees beyond the disturbing symptoms, which convince him that this is no case for him to be dealing with. He has not been taught simply to accept them as signs of deep stress. His anxious attention being focused on these archaic clinical side-effects, he may fail to grasp and deal with the present predicament. The trained pastor, by contrast, can take these added dynamic factors in his stride and make sense of them, whether he needs to interpret their origins to the troubled person or not.

FL's daily experience, over many years, beginning with

those when he used LSD to find a way through the most rigid personality defences, was that of listening to people in great emotional turmoil. He was familiar with the underlying territory and convinced of its importance. Nor did he believe it mattered only to those evincing nervous symptoms, as he explains in 1978:[2]

This dark mental land-mass of emotional and psychosomatic disorders exists in us all because actually stressful situations have impinged, too early, on vulnerable personalities. All of us are constitutionally prone to various *diatheses*, that is to say, to specific ways of tending to fall ill. Such stresses as occur affect different people in different ways. These two factors interact. The severity or not of the *proneness* or *diathesis*, and the severity or not of the stress, determine the outcome. What actually happened in infancy, as a result of these interacting forces, is preserved as repressed memories. They are like sensitive scars or injured limbs. They present, in adult life, as behavioural difficulties due to stressful conditioning – due, that is to say, to unfortunate experiences in infancy and what the person learned from those experiences about life itself.

Because this conditioning persists, they still feel that way about life. In that sense we should, but usually do not, think of them as *emotional learning problems* to be dealt with by *emotional re-education and re-training*. We slide [instead] into the medical model and think of them as illnesses or diseases . . . As a result, these human conditioning responses have become 'illnesses' requiring 'treatment'.

In 1981, he reaffirmed the point:[3]

The education of ourselves to help others in time of distress . . . inevitably has as its aim that of equipping us with the ability to perceive, within the confusion, what the main underlying causes are, and those contributory ones which will have to be dealt with to bring relief.

He insisted on the value for counsellors of understanding not only what current suffering is about but when and how it originated. For the pain and confusion going on in the person before them will seem less daunting if counsellors can see through to the much earlier stage of that person's existence, when such feelings were powerfully experienced but only dimly understood.

FL's model of the Dynamic Cycle is capable of describing at one moment the four-hourly cycles of infant feeding, at another a child's growth to maturity, at another an adult daily pattern of self-giving and replenishment. But each individual cycle was first traced out in what he called 'the womb of the spirit'. By this he meant, roughly, the first nine months of life, the period in which the newborn baby acquires its first sense of what the world is like. At this time the child is locked into such an exclusive relationship with its mother, or whoever gives it nurture, that it is hardly aware of any separateness between them. Ideally – and to begin with the foetal experience was assumed to have been one of near ideal bliss – the security of nine months in the womb was followed by the security of nine months of loving identification with the mother, accepted and sustained by her presence. As the body grew in the womb, so the spirit now grew in its sense of 'being' and 'well-being', so long as nurturing was generous and loving. The situation could become very different, however, if, in those same nine months, feeding problems developed or the quantity or quality of care was inadequate.

This view of the 'factors which make for a satisfactory sense of identity, selfhood and personal status' was one fairly generally accepted by child psychologists. It formed the foundations for the CT training from the beginning, and was illustrated by FL's astonishingly complex charts. These showed how interruptions to the healthy cycle may result in defensive reaction patterns which come into play throughout life whenever similar threats to the personality arise. As the foetus developed in the womb into a baby complete in all its parts, so the baby achieved its distinctive selfhood by its mode of responding to the pressures of life in its first nine months.

Where FL differed from many of his colleagues was in his insistence on the traumatic nature of birth itself:[4]

Support for the relevance of birth trauma has not come from many British psychiatrists or psychoanalysts, but has been given by one of the most distinguished of them, Dr Donald Winnicott. He writes, 'The . . . point that I want to make is that, in common with other analysts, I do find in my analytic and other work that there is evidence that the personal birth experience is significant, and is held as memory material.' He was also clear that intra-uterine experience prenatally was of importance to later development.

Many people with a premonition that their own births may have been decisive in determining the quality of their lives sought out FL in order to work with him. He wrote of this:[5]

It seems to me to be very useful and profitable to have experienced these highs and lows of our primal history. The high points are part of the wonderful cosmic creative activity of Christ. God looked upon his creation and behold, it was very good. He made it, and mammalian reproduction carries on with that making . . . The curse of the Fall for women is said to be 'greatly multiplied pain in childbirth, sorrow in giving birth', rather than the joy that might have been and, at times, still is. That 'greatly multiplied pain' does not end with the suffering of the mother. Every man woman and child came through the same place. The suffering of the baby in childbirth is in many ways far more acute than that of the mother. And, as we now know, it is totally remembered, though deeply repressed. Even in the nine months' growing in the womb there may be unimaginable sufferings and catastrophes. Certain it is that the foetus shares all the emotions of the mother, since the chemical substances which change within the mother's circulation with changing emotions, pass through the placenta into the foetus. Either it feels the same way, accepting either joy in its being there, or sorrow, resentment and hostility to, or total disregard of, its presence within. If an emotionally impoverished woman resents having to give anything to the foetus within her, the foetus is at the receiving end of these negative, non-giving and actually withdrawing feelings.

In the Primal Therapy workshops which he offered at Lingdale, in Nottingham, during which subjects sought to retrieve some of those 'first' or 'primal' experiences from around the time of their birth, evidence had begun to accumulate of stresses on the foetus well prior to the birth event. People 'reliving their memories' appeared to find themselves in a stage of foetal existence that went back to the earliest months of pregnancy. These findings caused a shift of emphasis in FL's thinking which disturbed many of his adherents and is still hotly contested. He stood by most of his earlier teaching – the nine months that followed birth had not lost their importance – but he had come to believe that the human spirit, as well as the human body, acquires many of its characteristics earlier still, within the womb. In 1981, the year in which his second book *Tight Corners in Pastoral Counselling*, which put forward this hypothesis, was published, he wrote:[6]

In 1966, in *Clinical Theology*, and . . . up until, in 1977, we were alerted to foetal dynamics, we saw and taught the applicability of the dynamic quadrilateral to the relationships of the baby to the mother in the 'nursing couple'. All this, of course, still stands.

. . . Through the mother's gracious and tender self-giving, an abundant, meaningful and satisfying selfhood is communicated, and is never lost, whatever follows . . .

In giving the name 'The Womb of the Spirit' to the nine months after birth, we used the analogy of the physical aspects of intra-uterine life, namely the utter reliance of the foetus on the intactness and unobstructed flow of oxygenated blood through the umbilical cord. The face-to-face, eye-to-eye bonding of the mother to the baby required the same intactness and total reliability. The analogy is still valid. [But] the term 'womb of the spirit' could now with more accuracy be transferred to the earlier developmental stage, within the first half of the nine months of pregnancy – which are the crucial ones – though extending throughout until birth.

Obviously, 'eye-to-eye bonding' and 'the mother's gift of her countenance' cannot take place within the womb, but their importance in the postnatal period remains paramount, as is shown in an earlier paper:[7]

After the birth, the baby needs to have the tension of those recent terrors smoothed away in loving contact with the mother's body. It needs to be bonded to the mother by face-to-face, eye-to-eye contact. Then it needs . . . to be taken to the breast for food. A number of young women who have had [in the process of 'reliving' their own births] the very distressing few hours in the birth followed by a sense of prolonged loneliness, have protested loudly at being taken immediately to the breast without first having a chance to establish a relationship and smooth out the tensions. If the loneliness after the birth is prolonged beyond endurance, there is a sense of being pushed to the edge of an abyss. Anxiety at separation increases while the courage and spirit of trust diminishes. At the point of despair and maximum panic there is a plunging over a cliff edge into the watery depths. The infant feels identified with nothingness, non-being, dread, and inhumanity. It may feel petrified, turned to dust, or into some lower form of insect life. Into the emptiness there is an inrush of negative archetypes, the 'terrible mother' images of witches, crabs, scorpions and terrifying birds. This is the original psychotic break. It is this to which some schizophrenic experiences return. This point is a kind of fulcrum within the soul, the worst point of pain, the result of 'god'-forsakeness . . .

> By the end of his life, in 1982, FL had concluded that experiences within the womb, in the process of birth, and in the initial months of life were all crucial to the development of the infant spirit. He even felt confident enough to pinpoint the area to which the psychic disturbances of many adults may be traced. (Newcomers to the subject may find this next passage easier to understand after they have read Chapter 4):[8]

There is one statement, not to do with bonding, on the [Womb of the Spirit] chart which obviously now demands correction. 'The roots of all the major neuroses – hysterical, phobic, conversion, schizoid, anxiety-depressive and obsessional – derive from separation-anxiety occurred in this phase' [i.e. the first nine months]. Some cases of each (though probably not of conversion reactions and severe obsessional neuroses) do take origin in severe deprivation of the mother's presence, leading, through separation-anxiety and panic, to mind-splitting dread. [However] the evidence gathered from 1200 and more subjects who have relived foetal distress in the first trimester [the evidence on which these conclusions are based] indicates that, if we are talking about the main roots of personality disorders and psychosomatic reactions, it is here we must look and not later.

> In retrospect, it seems surprising that psychologists should ever have supposed the infant spirit to be immune to prenatal influences, since folk-wisdom certainly maintained otherwise. Those who found no difficulty in accepting FL's later theories now saw the 'womb of the spirit' as embracing the entire prenatal, perinatal and early postnatal experience of the human organism, during all of which time it is subject

to primal hurts. And, this being so, an extra awareness was called for on the part of anyone offering care . . . In seminars at the Post Green Community in Dorset, members were told that they had to be alert not only to the quality of the parent/child relationship but to these further facts:

. . . When people are facing adult-life crises, if they can solve them with a minimum, or modicum, of emotion, using their reason, grappling with the realities of life . . . if they can solve the problem with such emotions as are appropriately attached to that situation, then well and good. But, if they can't, if you get a situation where somebody finds that this life-problem is insoluble – there is no way out and one is left totally on one's own and unsupported – then metaphor and conceptual distortions begin to operate.

It's as if the perplexed adult ego says, 'I can't solve this problem; it's insoluble.' And then something below says, 'You've met this before, you know.' . . . The memories of the past begin to reverberate, and will impose a perceptual mechanism, a way of patterning this thing, which says, 'It is as if I was way back there, in that earlier crisis.' And with this, of course, comes a de-skilling of the adult, who is no longer operating from his highest intelligence and his most discriminating emotions, because he is picking up a powerful impulse from the past which says, '. . . it's just like it was at the beginning, is now and ever shall be. And it doesn't get any better . . .'

And there is nothing he can do about it, except with some primitive child or foetal response way of coping, or opposing, or withdrawing, in much the same way as the primal event, the primal stress, the primal hurt was dealt with – highly undiscriminatingly, by one terribly unaware of what was really happening, in very poor contact with the outside world.

And all the more so if the thing that is resonating goes back to the womb. For there you haven't got sight or hearing, or language to discriminate with – or to be told by anyone what's happening or that it won't last always. It may be a temporary phase that the mother is going through, or that the family is going through, but the foetus does not know that. And therefore the whole problem of counselling is to recognize, and to give the person a grasp of how their life problem is complicated by the invasion of this primal material. To whatever problem there is in the present is added confusion and bewilderment as to why this present problem feels so all-or-nothing, so hopeless, so eternally bad, and why it is so difficult to cope with. [*Slightly edited*.][9]

... If [the mother's love and attention] is given to the full, then the baby has a strong sense of joy, of being, awareness, identity, and is able to fulfil the different tasks of babyhood ...

... The whole of our CT stuff is based on this sort of model being the norm. And what I am saying now is, the mere extension of this into prenatal areas only emphasizes that that is still the case.[10]

MATERNAL-FOETAL DISTRESS

At about that time, too, he wrote:[11]

I have no need to take back anything that was formulated ... in 1966 in the tome ... nor in the pamphlets ... I find it all, still, astonishingly true, well-conceived as theory and practice, and relevant resource material for Christian Pastoral Care. What I do have to admit has turned out to be a serious mistake was the assumption that the nine months of foetal development in the womb were free of significant incident, a blank without possibility of psychodynamic content ...

In *Tight Corners in Pastoral Counselling*[12] FL presented the fruits of his later years of work with people in distress. In the preface, he wrote:

For most of my psychiatric life I have been working in a half-light, oblivious of the earliest and severest forms of human pain. We have always known ... that infants suffered abysmally, and that human beings crawling out of their abysses into life have damaged perceptions, distorted goals and a lifetime bondage of primal fears. What we had not known, and even now are somewhat terrified to know as clearly and rigorously as in fact we do, is the contribution to this soul-destroying pain and heart-breaking suffering that comes from the distress of the foetus in the womb when the mother herself is distressed. The focus for psychopathology is now, for us, the first trimester of intra-uterine life. These first three months after conception held more ups and downs, more ecstasies and devastations than we had ever imagined.

He named this the 'Maternal-Foetal Distress Syndrome'

and described how he reached his conclusions in a paper written at about the same time:[13]

Some fundamental research into psychodynamic problems was carried out in the Clinical Theology Association by myself and two psychiatric colleagues from 1954 to 1969, utilizing LSD–25 as the psycholytic agent. The significance of the birth trauma in setting up the distorted perceptions typical of the claustrophobic syndrome was established and reported on in a paper read to the 2nd International Conference on Social Psychiatry. The use of LSD–25 was abandoned in 1969 since it became evident that a more accurate recall of perinatal experience, shorn of the over-elaborate symbolization and myth-laden quality associated with lysergic acid, could be attained by the deep breathing first suggested by Wilhelm Reich.

Recent work has shown that the pattern of deep breathing we stumbled upon, short, strong, full inhalation, followed by prolonged (and, with us, sonorous) exhalation, actually produces theta rhythm activity in the brain, and that the deliberate production of theta waves is an ideal bio-feedback method for reaching down to retrieve the memory of the earliest experiences which have been stored, repressed in the subconscious, having lost none of their power and vividness . . .

Employing these respiration patterns, our subjects had been able to retrieve perinatal and postnatal events with a precision and veridical assurance usually somewhat lost in psychedelic sessions. It did not occur to us to enquire whether the foetus could in any way be conditioned by intra-uterine events, or have any quasi or actual memory of [the] high pleasure or desperate distress of the mother during pregnancy. No theory put forth either by psychoanalysis or behavioural conditioning so much as suggested that it made any significant difference to the foetus or its later personality development whether it spent the nine months inside a deeply contented and cared for woman, protected from worry and fatigue, or shared the body of an anxious, distressed, harassed woman, driven to the point of suicide for herself or abortion of the hated product itself. We admitted no difference.

In 1977, a number of occurrences led us to suspect that powerfully impressive experiences from the mother and her inner and outer world did reach the foetus, defining its relation to intra-uterine reality in ways that persisted into adult life. We began seriously to test this hypothesis.

Our subjects were drawn from those who came on our three-day, then five-day, and now six-day residential workshops for Personal Growth and Primal Integration. Some are drawn from the helping professions, concerned to deal in some depth with a problem that stood in the way of satisfactory emotional functioning, either at home or at work. Others are wanting space and support while going through the mid-life crisis, a marriage conflict, or breakdown, or even retirement. Some are suffering from one of the disorders for which a psychiatric diagnosis is appropriate; it is not so much the abolition of their emotional pain that they seek, as for some more creative way of understanding and integrating it.

Others, family men of great integrity, come because they recognize that their inability to feel, to share the emotional life of their wives and children, is damaging those they love most. The once serviceable defences of the schizoid personality have become a burden also to them. At what level was the damage done which they wish now to repair, so as to feel again, and consent to be aware of, their own bodies, learning the language of the body for the first time, as a new commitment to intimacy becomes possible? . . .

The essential factor – present in some who are frankly patients, and absent at times in professional 'helpers' – is a paradoxical strength, caringly open to retrieve, accept and identify positively with all the weak and humiliated negativities of the hidden child of the past. If this adult capacity is not present when the week begins, most can readily learn it . . . facilitated by the competent modelling of others.

The pattern of activity during the workshop may be summarized in a short report made recently to the Assistant Director of the British Post-graduate Medical Federation, on whose behalf I conducted a three-day workshop . . .

After introductions and short statements of particular interests and expectations, Dr Lake outlined the clinical and experimental evidence for regarding the experience of the foetus, when the mother is distressed, as damaging to its emotional development and perceptual organization. Each member of the workshop was then given opportunity to speak of the aspects of their personality functioning on which they hoped to work. It became evident that four members wished to explore their own prenatal experience using this method, in a first group, which led to a further four doing the same on the third day.

The method of facilitating and its theoretical foundation was explained, so that this task could be undertaken by four members of the workshop in respect of the four who were working simultaneously. A further four undertook the verbatim recording of the session and supervised the tape recording of each subject's output. This occupied three hours on the Thursday and Friday afternoons, each followed by a feedback session. The connections between the presenting symptoms, or personality dynamics, and, on the one hand, the emotional and situational states of the subject's mother during the early months of that pregnancy, and, on the other, the sharply recollected impressions of intra-uterine existence which had been evoked, were made explicit.

The eight subjects were all able to make contact with their own early intra-uterine experience, stretching back in some cases to implantation, the blastocystic phase and even some sharp impressions of conception as a positive or very negative experience. The claim implicit in this work – that memory exists before the establishment of myelinated neurological circuits, as present in the microstructure and slow-wave activity in the synapses according to the holographic principle, and indeed earlier, in the protein molecular structures of the single cell and its successors – was abundantly substantiated. That a certain pattern of deeper breathing does constitute a biofeedback mechanism, producing theta wave activity, which acts selectively to bring apparently forgotten memories into consciousness, was confirmed in effect, though of course without electroencephalographic monitoring.

The threefold correspondence of (1) present symptoms, behavioural blocks, emotional colouring and persistent misperceptions of the environment with (2) the mother's state in these respects in the first trimester, and with (3) the recall by the subject of their experience, at certain recognizable junctures, during the life process through the nine months to birth and bonding, was strikingly apparent in all eight cases.

This research, over the past four years, based now on the records of over 1,200 subjects who have attended the residential workshops, has opened up an increasingly clear picture of the complexity of the interaction of the mother and the foetus . . .[14] Particularly during the first trimester of foetal life, it is most vulnerable to the influx of maternal distress, whatever its cause. By no means is it always due to her dislike of the pregnancy or to rejection of the foetus. We have encountered many in which her joy in bearing a child has been shattered by grief over the death of a parent or their fatal illness, or the worrying sickness of an older child, or anxiety that this one will miscarry as previous ones have done . . .

As soon as *implantation* has taken place the adult, to their own satisfaction in contact with their existence as embryo, will begin either to register the immersion and invasion of the mother's 'emotional biochemistry' as a good, comfortable medium to be in, or will complain of a bitterly cold or neglected, or even hated place. This may be in sharp contrast to the way in which they relived, or 'got in touch with', the *phase of the blastocyst*. For many, but by no means for all, this existence as a perfect sphere, free-floating and unattached, is one of sheer bliss.

An analysis, phenomenologically, of what several hundred of our subjects have reported while encountering this blastocystic phase, is identical with the descriptions of the mystical state, where it is monistic, a non-dualistic identification with transcendent being, awareness and joy. Some experience themselves here as brilliantly white, or gloriously blue, as containing all the secrets of the universe, as one with the ground of being, in total, blessed union with the whole universe. This is of clinical as well as of metaphysical interest. If a bad time follows in the first trimester, the embryo or foetus tends to use this state as one to which it, from time to time, will regress. It can be the basis of deistic fantasies in hypomanic states, and in marriage counselling its glory may invest, quite inappropriately, the object of infatuation, making her or him infinitely desirable, while the detested partner has, projected onto them, the horrific constrictiveness and invasiveness of the first trimester in a distressed or 'filthily angry' mother.

In testing this hypothesis, we have asked ourselves continually, how far could these remarkable responses be the result merely of suggestion on our part. We have to a great extent nullified this likelihood by having from four to eight subjects working in adjoining rooms at the same time. I rehearse, in a neutral, emotionally unbiassed voice, the undisputed facts of human development, the anatomy and the physiology of the meeting of the sperm with the ovum recently released from the ovary whose lifetime it has shared, to conception and cell division, to the morula and its hollowing out to form the blastocyst. After four days or so, some transitional message gets through, as if commanding it to 'get stuck in'.

At each phase so far described, eight subjects will have experienced and spoken quietly (though at times screaming in protest) about their eight quite different ways of responding to the shared 'talk-in'. That it is possible to make this kind of contact at all could be, perhaps, discounted as the product of suggestion. But if the responses are mere suggestion, based on my input, how can we explain away the wide differences in emotional quality and intensity, and the presence of so many and specific and individual details – which present themselves to the subject as vitally important insights based on what they themselves regard, with no kind of persuasion from me, as having some quality of memory or recollection?

The emotional patterning at the 'time' of implantation, whether delightfully competent, easy and rewarding when the task is completed, or difficult, 'like fighting to get through leather', or loathed as a disaster, taking place totally against one's will, or accepted under duress, as the only way to escape annihilation – each of these tends to be clearly recognizable as one of the powerfully shaping templates of later life experiences . . .

I have, from time to time, suggested to those who themselves have shared with me their recognition that so early an experience has been the basis of so much later misperception, that perhaps they are 'projecting back' some analogous later experience, drawing the primitive experience into the subsequent pattern. They are quietly adamant that first things come first, that the primary determinant in the shaping of their personal cosmos was indeed the most primitive one, and that I must be suffering from some strange perversity to suggest something so back-to-front and topsy-turvy. I suppose that my question must be based on an *a priori* assumption that no memory could possibly persist from the cells of the blastocyst and the primitive embryonic layer, even though every cell now present in our skin and central nervous system is derived from the ectodermal cells present on that occasion.

The most dramatic moment, in each prenatal integration session, whether it has occurred in Britain or Brazil, in Australia, India or Finland (and I confess to a fear that somewhere, sometime, nothing will happen when I reach this crucial point) is the time when I indicate that their growth, as embryo, has reached to about five weeks after conception.

Some groups have seen slides of a foetus at this stage, with the arms and legs appearing as buds. Describing the relation of the foetus to the umbilical vein, entering at the navel, and the two umbilical arteries which return blood to the placenta, I suggest that they take the offered hand of the facilitator and place three fingers over the navel. Continuing the deep breathing, I ask them to 'breathe up into their strength and the here and now'. Then, as they breathe out, to 'take the focus of awareness and attention down from the head, through the chest and down to the belly'. They give a resonant sound to the exhalation, emotionally neutral in character. I invite them to 'get in touch with what it was like to be in the womb at this stage, at the receiving end of all that their mother has to give'. If, as foetus, they make contact with any kind of feeling, they are to 'give it a voice', adding full expression of whatever the feeling is down there, to the resonant note as they breathe out fully.

At that moment, or within a few minutes, we are accustomed to hear as many distinct and totally different responses as there are subjects working. Some are silently, or with a gentle purring sound, celebrating the sense that this is a warm, comfortable and well-kept place to be in. Others are appalled that it is a cold, neglected place, somehow sensing that this is an alienated part of the mother's body, which she may even hate . . . At first the foetus tends to be aware that the mother does not know that it is present, yet often aware of wishing for recognition and a sense of being welcome . . .

All this was, and still is, met with a good deal of incredulity. I recall Frank saying to a conference group, as he sold us copies of *Tight Corners in Pastoral Counselling*, 'I didn't go looking for this stuff, you know. It's what I found.' In *Mutual Caring* he wrote:[15]

What is astonishing about the outcome of our exploratory workshops is the availability, in over ninety per cent of self-selected subjects, of specifically individual 'memory', with the power to relive and re-enact events and responses, evidently coded and recoverable in great detail, related to the first trimester. In most cases the worst of the distress is confined to this period. When the subjects, guiding themselves from month to month, pass into the period, some time in the second trimester, when, typically, even women who have been badly disturbed settle down to get on with having the baby, they report a decisive diminution of

acute distress. They enter upon a quite different sphere of existence, no longer dominated by the ubiquitous harassment of the
first trimester but for the most part well able to be coped with.
There is space and a new ability to move. Indeed, from many
reports it would appear that the utter terribleness of the early
months has already undergone an almost total repression . . .

> Further on, describing how writers such as Rilke and
> Camus have managed to translate the pre-verbal images
> that haunt 'schizoid personalities' into 'exquisitely accurate
> words', he concludes:[16]

It is all there, fully documented, but until now we have not
known *when* human beings were undergoing the experiences so
terrible as to warrant tortured language of this intensity. Now we
do, the extensions of the counsellor's ability to provide accurate
empathy, which is the core of his or her effectiveness, has reached
a new and authentic, because self-authenticating, depth of precision.

Knowing my own resistances, when these shocking facts began
to emerge, I do not imagine that the mere existence of this
information about the vicissitudes of the first trimester will
compel counsellors to rush to recognize this level of traumatic
fixation in their clients, and utilize its detail in sharpening the
accuracy of the interpretations on which empathy is ultimately
based. One can only fully empathize when one can conceive of
the strange images, sensations and emotions which the client is
impressing upon you, utterly real to them, as referring to experiences that actually happened . . .

Cell memory

> FL took pains to interpret the experiental evidence for the
> Maternal-Foetal Distress Syndrome gathered in his work-
> shops in the light of his own obstetric and laboratory experi-
> ence:[17]

All biological experimentation goes to show that if something
happened which, to the baby, is catastrophically frightening or
'being without a clear object' dreadful (to use Dr Winnicott's
phrase), the earlier it happens, the more it is 'etched' on the
personality. The evidence is that cell-memory long antedates the
development of memory based on fully functional (myelinated)

neurological circuits in the brain. The chemicals which mediate emotional states in the mother's body travel round in her circulation, so that many target organs in her body will add their contribution to the joy she feels or to the anger, exhaustion, despair, bitterness, or mixed feelings that she is experiencing. Whatever these feelings are, they become manifest to others in so many signs, gestures, expressions, and postures. They can have further evidences in the sensations, emotions, and symptoms that she herself can report.

Now all these circulating substances (in the category of catecholamines) pass through the placental barrier into the foetus. A few years ago, I could not have believed how fully and accurately adults can get in touch with what went on in the womb. But it is a fact that they can return to these intra-uterine states of mind to discover what the mother felt about them, their prenatal identity. They know very well whether they were wanted, or during which months of the pregnancy they were wanted (because sometimes this changes radically in the course of the nine months). All this is communicated from blood stream to blood stream. As the foetus lies in the womb, it is bathed in the love or hatred, fear or indifference, of the mother.

Birth, too, can add its chapter of shared accidents. The result of 'the Fall' for women is strangely confined to the business of having babies . . . When God first looked at his creation, including the remarkable arrangements for the masculine and feminine among mammals to engage in procreation, he said 'Behold, it is very good'. It works very well. After the Fall, this function is apparently the one which works particular havoc.

What we now realize is that this 'greatly multiplied pain' in childbirth is shared by the mother and the foetus, not equally, but quite differently. The mother has more stretching but the baby more crushing, more likelihood of death by asphyxia and shock, and *twenty to a hundred times more risk that it will be so severely damaged as to die*. Medical intervention reduces perinatal mortality (deaths just before, during, or after the birth) but, by the same token, more infants survive with traumatic memories.

These repressed emergencies and threats to survival, though immediately dissociated and split off from consciousness, will continue to provide a back-cloth of terror (often of a claustrophobic kind) whenever situations 'feel' the same. When, for instance, one is put 'under pressure' or 'pushed into a tight corner', 'committed to trying circumstances', 'faced with a decision with an uncertain outcome', 'driven round the bend', 'left with no room for manoeuvre', or 'pressed for time'.

The panic is much worse for the baby during its extrusion, because it cannot understand, as the mother can, what is going on. This sudden, unexpected change for the worse in its fortunes – this sudden expulsion from maximum comfort to maximum discomfort, with alarming sudden twists and turns on the way, collecting bruises and at times dislocations and fractures. All this is commonplace. So also are instrumental extractions or Caesarean sections. Asphyxia, felt as suffocation, is commonly very severe . . . All this is impressive stuff, etched upon the personality, taped and stored in cell memory to the last detail.

In his early teaching material, students learning about the reaction of infants in 'the womb of the spirit', would be surprised to hear that infants sometimes reacted so as to protect the mother. FL now saw this as happening even in the womb:[18]

. . . There can be a sense of *reversed flow*, the foetus feeling a need to give to this poor, weak mother. Well aware that it has little to give because little has been received, none the less there can be a fateful sense that 'it is my role to keep her alive . . .' Adults often feel that their parents cast them in the role of suppliers of love to loveless parents . . . What is hard to realize is that this reversed flow of love and caring, from child to parent, in a valiant attempt to get a small modicum of maternal tenderness, begins as far back as the interchanges which take place through the umbilical vessels, long before birth itself.

Just as beautiful nurturing experiences before, during, and after birth link up in the mind with the blessed archetypal images, greatly potentiating the simple facts of natural life, so bad relationships and terrible deficiencies in the same period evoke the negative and terrible archetypes. All the gods of the Hindu pantheon have their roots in the creative and destructive experience at the ground of our being and the roots of our human experience. They are just as recognizable as creative and destructive forces – with their corresponding images – when you are performing psychotherapy in the West, as they are in the religions of the East. It is just that in the West we need to help people to exteriorize them into a prolific galaxy of recognizable 'divinities'. The nearest we get to it in British ways of helping people to come to terms with these horrific images is through

Art Therapy . . . It is characteristic of deities which have their origin in perinatal experience that they are two-faced. The same forces that are gently supportive can turn into horrific crushers. And, in between the two, they are apt to be tricksters. The experience of birth seems to be full of nasty little tricks.

> For many of his critics, the sticking point was FL's insistence on taking foetal memory back almost to the point of conception, and crediting single cells with the faculty of memory. Yet he had been, in India, a parasitologist, and could speak with authority on the behaviour of cells:[19]

It is not uncommon . . . that human beings are able to go back to some kind of awareness of themselves when they were a single cell, that perfect sphere, the blastosphere, which travels down the fallopian tube into the womb in the course of almost a week. It then has quite a problem, sometimes, in gaining access to the uterine wall and establishing itself against the action of the immuno-suppressive mechanisms. The chemistry of this primitive cell mass has to handle the problems of ensuring that it will not be rejected as a foreign body. If, as I have done, you have spent many years examining single celled organisms such as the *Entamoeba histolytica*, and have observed how it expands its protoplasm under favourable circumstances and contracts itself into a cyst when life is tough, it isn't hard at all to attribute some kind of sensibility to the single cell. And even though now we each may number 10^{64} number of cells in our bodies, every one of them has derived its life, chromosomal material and memory from that original cell. That cell comes into its own in the womb, and often, 'its own does not receive it'. It becomes simply part of the next menstrual flow. Behind that is the void. It *seems* that Buddhism focuses its attention on events which are, to primal therapists, recognizable as those which belong to life in that first week after conception and back beyond it into the void out of which we came.

> In an interview reported in a special issue of *Self and Society*,[20] he is quoted as saying:

The catecholamines which mediate the emotions of the mother to herself – first through her own circulation – are so incredibly sensitive that they can differentiate, for example, between a double despair and a despair in the presence of a creative possibility. There is a big difference: the latter has an element of hope, the former hasn't – it is suicidal. All this comes through to the baby, or so it would seem from what people specifically recall in primal work . . .[21]

In 1980 he wrote of the Maternal-Foetal Distress Syndrome[22]

. . . This affliction is common among us . . . *caused, brought about* by the bitter distress of the mother, reacting to the badness of her past and present environments. It is not hereditary but acquired. It derives from the mother's feelings . . .

The physiological fact, that the bio-chemistry . . . of feelings of all kinds is transported, mainly by the circulation, to wherever it goes within the mother's own body, so that all of her feels it and many organs express it, is familiar enough and not specially damaging. It becomes pernicious . . . only when it travels to her pregnant womb and then across the placental membrane into the foetal circulation. There it *causes* and *brings about* all kinds of persecutory and annihilatory anxiety. This happens so early and is so incomprehensible and confusing to the foetus, can we not say that, for all practical purposes, 'God caused it', or 'an uncaused, innate death instinct caused it' or 'the genes carried it'? No, we cannot say any of these things, because such assumptions are not only without proof or evidence, they are disastrously damaging to the conduct of therapy and even worse for pastoral care.

. . . The evils with which the mother is surrounded, and with which she may be bravely coping, are funnelled into the foetus. Much that is bad may be filtered off by her courage and faith, but the shock which recruits her courage is itself transmitted . . .

In biblical terms, the sins of the fathers – all the chaos into which social organization and relationships are precipitated by human sin – fall particularly heavily on those who most need peace and security around them, the pregnant mothers . . . often not protected but rather threatened by social structures when they need help most . . . This is the picture that emerges from [our] research, confirming earlier psychoanalytic work.

Convinced as he was of its value for 'sharpening the accuracy of the interpretations on which empathy is ultimately based', FL always described the Maternal-Foetal Distress Syndrome as a hypothesis to be checked and tested.[23] Meanwhile, counsellors do no harm if they listen for resonances from a dark, warm, watery place which may have been anything but total bliss.

BREAKDOWN OR BREAKTHROUGH

Reliving primal memories is, more often than not, deeply disturbing, which raises fears that self-exploration of this kind may lead to breakdown. FL saw the re-owning of the weakness and darkness within ourselves as not without risk – and he always made it clear that we need our defences and must be free to relinquish them in our own good time – but as a necessary preliminary to a breakthrough into strength and insight, the true light of day. He wrote:[24]

What is miscalled 'breakdown' may be the result of a strong and true spirit's attempt to face too much human reality.

The distinction between a constructive disturbance in a person, which may be the preliminary to new life, and a destructive disturbance, which requires psychiatric help, has been dealt with in his books. In Edinburgh[25] he described it in terms of 'spiritual transition':

A major transition may occur in the course of the spiritual life, . . . remarked upon, I think, in all religious systems. When it occurs in Christians it seems to be correlated with this transition in the life of Christ, from active action to action through passivity. It is a change from doing to bearing. In the early stages of our spirituality we are given, by grace, many activities along the lines of our vocation, with a lively sense of the fruits of the spirit, the power, peace and joy of God's presence in our lives . . . During the transition there is characteristically a diminution to the point of absence of these subjective feelings about God's action in us, which have hitherto brought us such pleasure and joy. Faith must now persist without faith feelings. Our joy becomes hidden, and we must permit it to be hidden with Christ in God. The Holy Spirit no longer garrisons our hearts and minds from their own disturbing depths, but rather seems to be concerned to drag them [the feelings] out into the light of consciousness. We are troubled by inner fears and negativities of which we may have only childhood memories or hints in dreams. An unfamiliar darkness descends upon the spirit which has nothing at all to do with sin nor backsliding, and everything to do with the healing and purgation of the roots of evil, distrust, doubt and dread within us. If wise pastoral care, that knows these things, is not present, what ought to be a creative breakthrough can too easily be interpreted as loss of faith, leading into, in many cases, a nervous breakdown and the necessity for psychiatric care.

It is vital to the pastoral understanding of troubled people, going through darkness and doubt in middle life, that we remember, as an extension of Freud's dictum, that the traumatic and disturbing elements of the unconscious (all the buried memories, that is, of distrust and doubt of the parents who are the gods of infancy, through whose unwitting failures the dreadful has too often happened) can be expected to return to consciousness, not only at times of ill-health, whether it be spiritual, social, mental or physical, in the form of breakdown, but equally at times of abundant health in all areas of man's being . . . At such times it would seem more sensible to speak, not of breakdown but of breakthrough. This is as creative an experience as the other is destructive. But in both cases there is something sacramental about it, an outward and visible sign of an inward and invisible disgrace.

The first response of the tissues to a deep shrapnel wound is to wall it off *in situ*, so that it cannot spread infection and death to the whole body. But then, as years pass, and health is restored to a high pitch, the tissues will work this foreign body to the surface, until it presents under the skin, and asks, as it were, for removal. Similarly, in abundant health, the attics and basements of the human spirit are being emptied of old junk. This is a phenomenon both of nature and of grace. It is certainly the Holy Spirit's work.

The irony of the situation is that too many ministers, hearing a hint from this or that parishioner of strange, disturbing feelings and fantasies that are tumbling out into the front hall of his mind, can only interpret such *dreadful* dark or dirty contents as evidence of backsliding under the old terminology or a nervous breakdown under the new. Treating his parishioner as he treats himself, the minister insists that Christians don't have such thoughts. They must be returned promptly to the attics and basements from which they emerged. That it is of the very nature of sanctification, as a process of eradication of evil of every kind, first to insist that it be looked at steadily, accepted as one's own, and then dealt with under the Cross, of this the minister seems to have no knowledge.

If his anxious exhortation fails to effect the cure of re-repression, he hands the patient over to his general practitioner. This good doctor, pressed for time, and maybe also uninstructed in the differential diagnosis between breakdown and break-through, will attempt to seal up the attics and the basements of the mind with pharmacological glue. Minister and doctor are here acting in collusion with Western man's fear of the unknown dark continent within him, where death of the self in dread sits like a bird of prey, blindfolded, for the time being, by the owner, but biding its time, waiting its chance to attack again.

4

The Defence of the Personality – Part I

MURDERING THE TRUTH

As we have seen, the reaction of the human organism, at
the very start of its existence, to physical and emotional
pain or deprivation is to repress all memory of it. Frank
Lake sometimes described this as the 'vital' or 'pervasive'
lie, or, even more dramatically, 'murdering the truth':[1]

. . . As soon as the tragedy of human life impinges upon the
infant, indeed upon the foetus still within the womb, the truth
of what has happened is immediately murdered by repression
and turned into a lie which denies that it ever happened. Christ
Jesus insisted that the Pharisees, the exemplary religious people
in his own environment, were encapsulated in lies, with a lie at
the core of the whole religious programme. Their response to
him was to seek to kill him. 'You seek to kill me because my
Word finds no place in you.' (John 8:36) 'You seek to kill me,
a man who has told you the truth which I heard from God.'
(John 8:40) Christ follows this by a classical statement on the
effect of repression and the defence by incomprehension: 'Why
do you not understand what I say? It is because you cannot
bear to hear my Word. You are of your father the Devil, and
your will is to do your father's desires. He was a murderer from
the beginning, and has nothing to do with the truth, because
there is no truth in him. When he lies, he speaks according to
his own nature, for he is a liar and the father of lies. But because
I tell you the truth, you do not believe me!'
. . . When mental health is defined socially as exemplified by
the representatives of the dominant culture, whenever anybody
challenges this, they deprive him of nationality, and certify him
as insane. This is exactly what the Jews did to Jesus. 'Are we
not right in saying that you are a Samaritan . . .' (therefore
outside the covenant wherein the knowledge of God was given)

65

'and demon-possessed?' (John 8:48) Feeling 'stoned' by the pressure under which Christ's strong words placed them, 'they took up stones to throw at him'. (John 8:59)

This, quite simply, is the cost Christ had to pay for promoting radical mental health. I doubt whether the cost is any cheaper nowadays . . . And still, the heart of religious man is the place of the deepest lie, because it encourages the highest pride.

The mental health of the average man, in this view, is a life lived over the top of a tissue of closely woven lies, a fabric of falsehood . . . Therefore, the line between the 'normal' person and the 'neurotic' is not that the normal personality can function without intrinsic falsehood whereas the neurotic person cannot. Quite the contrary.

We call a person 'normal' if the self-deception that he uses to repress, deny, displace, and rationalize those basic wounds that are ubiquitous in human beings from babyhood works quite well. He is 'normal' in so far as his defences against too much painful primal reality are as successful as (all unbeknown to the person himself) they are meant to be.

How we cope with those 'basic wounds' depends on the time, nature and extent of the primal injuries and on our own physical constitution and inherited characteristics. But, while each of us defends against pain in an individual way, building up, through our earliest experiences, a unique pattern of reactions that comes into play whenever we feel threatened by circumstances or events, the kind of neurotic symptoms we exhibit under extreme pressure fall into recognizable categories. We may become deeply depressed, intolerably demanding, desperately alienated, unbearably anxious, or absurdly suspicious. Or we develop bodily symptoms for which there seem to be no physical causes. Our doctors then describe us as Depressive, Hysteric, Schizoid, Anxiety-prone, Paranoid, Hypochondriacal, and so on.

These reaction patterns and how they come about are fully described in CTA teaching materials and in FL's books, and it is there that readers should look for a fuller understanding of them. Here, drawing on assorted unpublished materials, we can only offer a sampling and, at times, a fresh slant. Two of the following passages are taken from a series in the magazine *Renewal*, where, in 1976–77, FL acted as a sort of agony uncle under the heading 'Frank Lake replies'. Christians who had experienced a resurgence of faith were discovering that the old Adam could still create trouble within. The remainder are from assorted articles, lectures, pamphlets and tapescripts.

THE DEPRESSIVE REACTION PATTERN

In his Edinburgh lecture[2] he had this to say:

... Psychodynamically speaking, the personality structures enshrined in the average church-goer and in the more respectable clergy tend to be either depressive or obsessional. In terms of personality orientation, such people are rooted in an attitude that clings to the past, or some aspect of it, as basically good. This is in sharp contrast to the hystero-schizoid dynamics which ... are in blind flight from the memory of total badness, of the splitting of personality in pain at the point where it was necessary to establish trust ... By contrast, pre-depressive personalities still cling to the past and its structures in Church and state. They manifest a sound sense of conservatism, the desire to defend the *status quo*, the idealization of the Church or state to which they belong, a need to hide its bad sides, and therefore a fundamental rejection of any dialectical ecclesiology. From psycho-dynamic studies we know that the unattractive hinterland of depression, as Luther knew so well, is marred by repressed rage and hate, lust and envy, anxiety, distrust, doubt, and even, at times, despair. But all this must be shut away, however wearisome the internal conflict becomes.

There is a gospel to be proclaimed here, an authentic evangelism for the unconscious continent within the depressed man and woman within the pew. It is a *theologia crucis*. The fixated image of god, small 'g', in depressive people is that of the stern, condemnatory parent who approves only of those who keep the law, who accepts the sinner only when full reparation has been made, and who demands a constant flow of good works. The pastoral counsellor's task is, with the minimum of words, and relying mainly on his own embodying of the unconditional acceptance of Christ, to bring this work-weary man or woman to the place of rest, as the writer to the Hebrews speaks of it.

I do not know of any situation which so dramatically calls out for, and responds to, our central doctrine of justification by faith ... The pastoral care of sufferers from reactive depression is most rewarding.

As for the internalized rage, kept under at great cost and

wearisome effort by the neurotic conscience, the counsellor follows Luther's line. A pastor friend of his came to Luther in deep depression . . . Luther went straight to the core of the depression, the unadmitted rage. 'Are you angry with me,' he asked, 'or with God, or with yourself?' The murderous rage is so strong that to save others, a man may kill himself. The Cross of Christ is begging the depressed religious man to trust him sufficiently to offer the murderous rage to him not just mentally, but physically, to direct the evil on to him whose work is to take away our evil, at the cost of his own death. As Robert Leighton, once minister of Addington and later Archbishop of Glasgow, wrote to a depressed woman, 'I bid you vent your rage in the bosom of God.'

The lusts, too, which are largely fantasy matters, can be spoken of. They often provide the material of confession in depressed people. The Christian pastor takes his cue from Christ's ready acceptance of the three women taken in adultery. Under the Cross such things are no barrier to fellowship. Here there is ample scope for evangelism and pastoral care in a Christianly modified psychotherapeutic approach to the depressed, at least to those who can still talk about themselves.

Former seminar members may recall taking part in the 'Sixteen person role play', in which the turmoil of one depressed person is re-enacted. Four members are needed to repress the underlying rage, lust, anxiety and despair, while four more ensure that the public face expresses the exact opposite of the 'truth in the inward parts'. It demonstrates how much vital energy the depressed person expends in the task of denying negative feelings and in trying to be 'good'.

In the following extracts from *Renewal* magazine, FL looks at problems of repressed anger. A 'composite question' is followed by his reply. Both are somewhat abridged:[3]

The question: What has happened to make me feel so much worse as a person just at the time when God is so real to me and has been showing himself and his love to me as never before? All kinds of secret sins and shortcomings seem to be staring me in the face. That this should happen just when I have come alive spiritually in so many joyful ways doesn't make sense . . . In particular I am at a loss to know how to deal with all the anger that seems to be welling up inside me. I feel it would be discouraging, particularly to the younger members of our group, if I spoke about this openly. Others might get it out of proportion . . . What should I do about these apparently contradictory directions I seem to be going in?

After restating the question to show the force of the dilemma, FL replies:

Let's look at your background as a person. In the years before you came into this renewed experience in Christ, were there times when you became rather depressed? Did you react to disappointment or injustice, not by showing your feelings openly, but by going quiet, withdrawing into yourself, feeling unaccountably tired, and becoming generally depressed – but certainly without any show of anger or open resentment?

Very probably you did. Religious people, and even conscientious people who have no contact with the Church at all, are prone to depression, as well as disappointment, when things don't go as well as they have expected.

If, as I expect, this is the case with you, then the anger is the honest presence, in your conscious mind and self awareness, of the anger that was actually present within the depression. Anger is present in every depressed person but it is covered up by mental defence mechanisms that can be summed up in the word 'guile'.

These mechanisms are established very early in life. All sorts of things happen to us in babyhood that make us angry. It just isn't possible for mothers or fathers to meet all our needs. Angry crying is the natural response. Most mothers are not threatened when their babies react to disappointment in this way. They accept it, and so the baby can accept it, as a shareable emotion. It is not a pleasant feeling, but the baby can be honest about it, mother permitting. The competent mother is just concerned, but not put out, by the anger shown when she has to leave her baby to attend to other things for a while.

Some parents, however, cannot tolerate anger in their offspring. They feel guilty and depressed enough already, and pushed to the limit of endurance. To have to listen to the angry crying of an obviously unhappy and discontented baby, when you've already done all you can think of and have tried to meet its round-the-clock needs, is too much. So an angry voice is heard, 'Oh, shut up! Stop your noise, can't you? Be quiet!' Accompanied perhaps by an angry slap to reinforce the threatening tones of the angry voice. This teaches the infant a prime lesson about life. Parents can be angry. That is their right. You the baby must never be angry. You have no right to be angry. Look at all mummy is doing for you. Be thankful that some of your needs are being met. And if you feel angry that many more have not, remember there's a war on inside mummy and she'll go to pieces if you don't shut up. So split off your anger at unmet needs and develop a placid exterior. Guile pays. It makes friends even for babies and it influences people. Hide away wrath. Hope fervently that it will never be uncovered . . .

The more strenuous the guile the greater the parental reward. And since, at this level of experience, parents are confused with God, religion, which claims to speak for God, and religious groups get into the bad habit of rewarding the concealment of anger which exists, by means of guile.

The God of the Psalmists speaks in a totally different way. 'Blessed is the man in whose spirit there is no guile.' When we come to the New Testament we learn that the character of God is such that even such violent anger in us as leads to the murder of his son on the cross, does not prevent him, in exactly the same moment that we prove that we are his murderers, from declaring that we are also his beloved. 'Father forgive them,' he said, as they drove in the nails, 'they do not know what they are doing.' It was not their own anger that the hammering hands of the soldiers expressed. It was the anger of others, particularly of the religious, that gave murderous force to the nails.

The God and Father of our Lord Jesus Christ does not accept you, my friend, because you have a long and successful record as a religious man in the guileful concealment of rage. Nor does he reject you when the anger stored up since infancy in your hard-pressed body bursts out into consciousness as the armour of guile is shattered by the Spirit of Truth . . .

FL then looks at other possible roots of anger in a difficult birth, feeding problems, or the lack of a loving mother.

Religion keeps down the hot fires of anger (and indeed of loving) by inducing a state of permafrost. Weeds cannot grow, but no more can genuine fruits. We become what Bishop Taylor Smith used to call 'Christmas Tree Christians'. We have no roots and no fruit. We tie attractive baubles of good works done for public admiration on to the dead branches, and are angry if they are not noticed and approved of . . .

This depth anger, which surfaces in Christians as part of the renewal or spring-cleaning of the Christian, is so much a part of the Holy Spirit's own anger, at the injustices suffered by little children, that if there is any difficulty in 'getting it out' in the ordinary way, it will usually surface strongly and authentically when expressed in tongues. We praise him in tongues. We can praise him with our anger in tongues because this wrath is the wrath of the Lamb. It is part of the saving indignation of God against all that blocks our way to his life and love in its fullness.

The suggestion that his questioner might release his anger 'in tongues', if self-revelation in intelligible language feels too risky within the Christian group, shows FL sensitive to the magazine's particular readership. He doesn't attempt to enjoin on them the degree of open sharing of the dark side of themselves that he would have looked for in his small groups at Nottingham. He offers, instead, an acceptable alternative. (Of his own involvement in the Renewal we shall have more to say in the final chapter.)

In a later issue of the magazine[4] he tries to meet the angry objection that the Christian ought not to express anger openly but repent of it, ending with these words:

Here most 'religion' based on 'what I ought to do' parts company with Christian, Christ-based living. The only 'ought' left to the Christian is that of relating first of all to Jesus, of going straight away, without the delay of a preliminary moral wash-and-brush-up, to the Christ and his cross. This is, to me, the 'repentance' and '*metanoia*', or change of mind, we most urgently need, namely to change from our habitual tendency to deal with our 'badness' by telling ourselves what we ought to do about it, in order to please God, rather than please God at once, by taking the whole bellyful of our 'badness' direct to the 'scapegoat' God the Father has himself appointed, and off-loading the lot obediently onto the Son.

When the Spirit comes to convict us of sin, it is not *primarily* to tell us that anger is wrong, or sex is wrong, or over-eating is wrong, or destroying other people with bitter scorn is wrong, or smoking is wrong, though he may well point to any of these as grieving him. Primarily he convicts because we do not believe in Jesus. It is being related to Jesus, having the Spirit of Jesus in us, which is our salvation, not freedom from bad habits. That follows. It does not precede.

71

Earlier we quoted FL as saying that the inner dynamics of most church-going Christians are basically depressive, leading them to want to prove themselves by good works, adherence to the law, and denial of any impurity or pain within themselves. Members of the clergy and other pastoral counsellors need to have confronted their own inner darkness so as to be able to hear, accept and stand alongside the sufferer without being overwhelmed by the other's pain. But depressed people, who tend to blame themselves for their misery, make far fewer demands on the counsellor than do those who defend themselves with a different set of inner dynamics, as we shall see in the passages that follow.

THE HYSTERIC REACTION PATTERN

. . . The core of the hysterical position . . . is the mental pain of separation of the infant from the presence and countenance of the mother or of a substituted personal source of being.[5]

The person whose infant experience, in the Womb of the Spirit, was of separation from the source of life through the absence of the source person, or through being left to scream and cry overlong before anyone came to bring relief, is imprinted for life with the expectation that no one loves or feeds, comforts or helps, willingly and spontaneously. And yet, to be left unnoticed and unattended is, as it truly was for the infant, to die. Such a person cannot endure solitude and, particularly in times of stress, feels impelled to cling to anyone who seems likely to provide help by any means possible. In the pamphlet issued to Clinical Theology Seminars[6] in the sixties and seventies, the hysteric reaction is contrasted with the depressive in this way:

The depressive personality pattern shows compliance, meekness, and an inability to make even a necessary degree of self-affirmation. These are not virtues, arising freely from love of others, but part of the compulsion to deny that this self feels now, or has ever felt, even as a baby, a tremendous all-embracing rage against important people, from mother and father onwards. Again, where prudishness and joyless, judgemental morality form a part of the pattern, . . . this is a denial of the fact that the infant had turned to libidinal fantasies as a defence against the terrors of separation from the mother.

72

When a baby's response to separation anxiety is rage and libidinal fantasy, we call this an *active* reaction. The baby to whom this experience comes is, of course, in a state of weakness, need and passivity. He cannot imagine meeting his needs from his own resources. But there is in him an element of strength that is enough to make him long to be able to compel his parents to submit to his wishes. Being a pigmy among giants, he can do very little, but he can have desperate fantasies of successful aggression against their 'bad' aspects, or of successful seduction of their 'good' ones. In fantasy, his puny strength is no longer impotent but devastatingly effective to destroy and conquer. That is why he is so frightened and horrified by it, and powerfully splits it off and rejects it. Love, too, may play a part in him. His instinct to respond expectantly to other people can lead him to use this small element of strength to keep rage and lust under the control of his super-ego, and to go on doing this in later life.

Without this element of strength, before perhaps it has had time to develop, or if it has been dissipated by illness, the story is different. We can no longer talk of the baby having a sense of his power to command and control. So, even if rage is part of the emotional content of separation anxiety, he mounts no fantasy attacks on his frustrating parents. Again, when he flees to libidinal fantasies, these are too weak to keep terror at bay. Passivity here is total, and we mark the distinction by calling this a *passive* reaction to separation anxiety.

This absence of 'activity' in the primary experience of dread, leads to the formation of a reaction pattern that is markedly different from the depressive one. It is characterized by compulsive activity of an attention-seeking sort. Although this activity may be disguised as compliance and submissiveness, these are means to an end, which is complete control of a source-person who is not to be allowed to escape. Although it may be disguised as love, there is no deep-rooted concern for others playing its part in the super-ego to curb and restrain the destructive effects of this clamour for attention. Expedience is the foundation for morality, motive and act. We call this active kind of compulsive behaviour the hysterical personality pattern.

For such people, no amount of family love and public admiration, or of time and attention devoted to them in the doctor's surgery or pastor's study, wipes out the sense that no one cares. FL has told the story of a doctor who emigrated to Australia to escape from the demands of an hysteric patient, and of a client who was discovered to be seeking help from no fewer than six clergymen, all of whom were nearing the point of breakdown! Similar situations can develop with bank managers and solicitors, all assuming themselves to be the only source of hope or understanding, and all sworn to secrecy. In CT seminars, the problem that most often arises, when members are invited to present a situation that is causing them particular difficulty, is one with a person of this kind, whether it is a parishioner, client or family member. And there is no easy answer, because the person's desperate and very real need of help gives what FL has called 'power and malignancy' to their demands, which may lead conscientious Christians into avoidance ploys quite alien to their generous natures. During seminars at Post Green, FL talked about how to give care without loss of one's own integrity:[7]

. . . What happens, usually, with an hysterical personality is that they get their foot in the door, you didn't want to see them . . . you were supposed to be doing something else . . . And they charge in, and [you] having, as it were, done something to mollify them or satisfy them, if that is possible – at least you'll be rid of them and hopefully they won't come back again. You see? And they know this. They know that if they have a tough enough story, you'll give them another hour, but always unwillingly. So nothing you ever give has been given through love or freedom. And therefore the hysterical child [in them] knows perfectly well this is not love I am getting. It's only the end product of my skill in manipulating people, and I despise the bastard, anyway. And you learn that, too. *So it is absolutely vital that what you do, you do freely. What you arrange, you arrange freely.* And that you don't (in the hope that they will never come back) leave them without an appointment . . . Then, if they ring up in between, you listen politely for three or four or five minutes, and say, 'Yes, that's something which obviously has tipped you over into your child-place again, that very frightened place, and I'm glad you were able, as an adult, to get on the phone and talk about it to me. Let's go over it in proper detail next time, at our next meeting. Till then, we can leave your adult in good charge of this situation. Let your adult have some dialogue with your child about it. Talk to the child in pretty much the same way as I would.'

You see? And they accept that, and they know that this has

only been a reasonable, not an unreasonable, invasion of your time, the kind of invasion that anybody might make. And it's all right. But the important thing to say is, 'Your adult's in charge of this.'

And, equally important, the counsellor remains in charge of the relationship. In a seminar in Finland, he was replying to a question about the comparative value of primal therapy and charismatic healing, which may have contained some flattery of himself, since he answered it in this way:[8]

. . . If anybody ever tells me I'm the most wonderful understanding person they have ever met, I begin to be very suspicious, because I wonder where I am being led and I have to establish control. Because what we call the 'hysteric' patient is fighting for control of the therapeutic situation. They do not trust anybody, but their child has become devilishly skilful at getting therapists into all the stupidest places that they are capable of getting them into. It is as if they are saying, 'Well, at least if I can't be happy, I'll be successful, and my success will be proving how many fool therapists there are around the place' . . . and they can find an inexhaustible source of fool therapists! Now that is somebody who is regressed, but whose adult has been twisted into the service of the regressed child.

What you are trying to do both in primal therapy and in what you might call 'charismatic therapy', the healing of the memories, is this. You are first of all building up people who are as adult as they can possibly be, people who take responsibility for themselves, . . . who recognize that everybody has got time limits and who, when they are given time, use it well. They are thoroughly aware that they are not a special case, for special treatment, but just one ordinary person with a lot of others . . .

You must realize, you see, that the Holy Spirit is giving people increasing sensitivity to these things. But there are some charismatics who despise anything that you have to learn, as it were, about group dynamics and psychology. And my experience of them is that they are always on a bit of an ego trip and that they are always damaging somebody when they do that.

In the pamphlet quoted earlier, Andrew Todd alludes to what may happen when the primal deprivation is so great as to drive the nascent ego up to or beyond the margin of its tolerance of mental pain:[9]

When we come to study the schizoid reaction pattern, we shall see that such *transmarginal* experiences [*See Ch 1*] can set up personality patterns which have the goal of avoiding relationships instead of seeking them. In fact, more often than not, we find that people whose predominant pattern is hysterical show traces of schizoid detachment in some aspects of their compulsive behaviour. This suggests that they have had some encounter with the experience of uttermost dread beyond the margin of tolerance of mental pain. Nevertheless, their basic over-riding goal has remained person-seeking, and so we continue to describe their behaviour as hysterical.

THE SCHIZOID REACTION PATTERN

FL took up this theme in his Edinburgh lecture:[10]

A primal injury to the personality has split its roots into two quite separate systems. One grows up to seek light and air in the world outside the self. This is the extraversial aspect. It depends on sensory input for its experience of reality. The tree from the other root grows up into the world of the mind, the inner world of reflection, reason, intellectual and mystical resources. This is the introversial aspect. It lives by detachment, in fact it created itself by reflection. [Feeling that] nobody . . . responded to its basic need of others, it resolved to live by self-consciousness. Being essentially self-creating, it continues to be self-subsistent. It feeds upon itself, turned in upon its own mental processes. Here it finds all the reality it dare recognize. The outer world is admitted to a kind of reality only after it has been processed by the thinker, deprived of its unique and actual existence, and admitted only when it has been reduced, or elevated (it depends on the point of view) to a concept familiar to the thinker's framework of thought.

Whereas the extraverted aspect of the personality cannot wait for the coming of attentive persons, with their faces indicating concern, such a contingency would be terrible, literally unthinkable, to the introverted person. Why is this? In brief, because it was when this same person, within the first year of life, before the transition which makes separation from the mother tolerable, was waiting for the re-establishment of personal life by the coming of the mother . . . there was a terrible failure to establish connections in the external world. The baby lives in the light of the mother's countenance. The helpless baby, crying in the night, utters its urgent prayer to god – small 'g' – to show the light of his or her countenance. Waiting time becomes dying time. Faith, hope, love, trust, courage and all the powers of the spirit decline until they come to the end of their tether. Anxiety, mental at first perhaps, but speedily involving the whole body in physical distress, rises to the ultimate panic of separation.

Here there is a margin of tolerance, a cliff-edge of possibility of trying to sustain the synthesis. Then, at a point determined by constitution, heredity and recent experience, the spirit cracks under the strain. The heart breaks and there is a falling headlong into the abyss of dread and non-being. The self is annihilated. God is dead. Prayer is not answered . . . There is an identification, not with human beings, but with non-being . . . Those in whom this experience is being relived feel that they are degraded to lower forms of life, to the insect or the worm. They may feel petrified, turned to stone, or pulverized to dust. Yet this is an experience of unconditional badness which registers in the infant mind as a kind of guilt. Guilty of dust and sin. 'Affliction', the word Simone Weil uses for this state of mind, makes its most innocent victims feel the most guilty of all . . .

This is . . . the area of the demonic, of the overwhelming floods, the arid deserts, the hell-fires and tortures of which the Psalmists speak. It is a pity that those who still sing the psalms have no idea of the experience to which they refer. I have sometimes wondered whether to suggest that one of my patients should visit his minister indicating that he is suffering from a bad attack of Psalm 88, and cannot readily say the Gloria at the end of it.

The instinctive response of the human mind to this occurrence is to split it off from consciousness and to repress it as soon as possible. And yet it remains the most potent source of dynamic drive throughout life.

Later in the same lecture[11] he says:

I have so far scrupulously avoided any use of medical diagnostic terms. But they occur so commonly now in the dailies and the weeklies that I hope you will not take it amiss if I mention that those who are in flight from social contact, into withdrawal and introverted activity within the mind, are often referred to as suffering from schizoid personality disorders. Those who are still clinging to life in the external world of material things and of people, are referred to as suffering from a hysterical personality

disorder. In the conceptual framework to which I have introduced you these are both forms of flight from the central core of
dread. Since both co-exist in all those who suffer from one or
the other, we can speak of hystero-schizoid personality problems.
These have, I believe, always been characteristic of the Gentile
world . . .

> FL wrote so extensively about 'schizoid affliction' that selec-
> tion is difficult, but there are memorable passages in a
> sermon preached at Great St Mary's Church, Cambridge,
> in 1963, on 'Christ the Therapist'. His text was John
> 16:16–24. 'In a little while you will *not* see me any longer,
> and again in a little while you *will* see me, because I am
> going to my father':

. . . If we are to speak of Christ as therapist in this place, it is
upon this gravest of all problems of personality that we must
concentrate. Whether it disguises itself in inordinate, narcissistic,
solipsistic self-love and admiration, or has begun to wear thin
in a poetic orgy of self-pity, or has advanced aggressively to a
bitter self-hatred or shrunk away through a nauseating self-
loathing into terminal apathy, it is the same affliction. Technically we speak of it as *the schizoid personality disorder*. The man or
woman who suffers from this condition is alienated from human
life in the ordinary family sense. He cannot in depth define
himself confidently by reference to a welcoming human face and
say, 'I was loved, therefore I am', because human mother-love
failed him crucially . . .
    . . . All moves towards commitment are liable to provoke deep
anxiety. The prospects of the bonds of matrimony may cause
reverberations and shudderings and uncanny reactions of dread
and compulsive withdrawal as from terrible bondage. One or
other area of life, in which unhurt people can commit themselves
to other persons closely, must always remain barred to the truly
afflicted person. Some repress their fear of the woman, and
marry . . . Others project their commitment anxiety, as rational-
ists and positivists tend to do, on to commitment to God. The
very idea of trust in a source of personal being outside one's
own produces an uncanny deep-down shudder reaction which
paralyses actual movement towards God, though it may, by
reaction, intensify argument and study and expertness of intellectual knowledge about him.
    By avoiding deep personal commitment and engaging in a

hectic life of activity or a rigid pattern of conformism, whether it be religious, high or low, or political, left or right, or the intensive pursuit of power or pleasure, but particularly of knowledge, a man may ward off the dreadful awareness that as a person related deeply to persons he does not exist at all . . . He may compensate for his emptiness and lack of community by solitary creativeness . . . but he does this in an ivory tower built over unvisited dungeons of despair. If his defences break down, as so often happens when the intensive structuring of school examinations is taken away at the university, he is liable to break down in a crisis of personal emptiness, meaninglessness, or of utter hollowness or (as we would say technically) of identification with non-being.

Then, in spite of all his intellectual gifts, he feels, as a person, worthless, a burden to himself and others. His introspection is in complicity with his illness and, the more he searches into the depths of himself, the barer the ontological cupboard is found to be. Psychoanalysis, purely as analysis, in devoting itself to introspection, does but 'feed the foul disease'. His whole mental life, like Hamlet's, sinks into a soliloquy on the possibilities of ending it all by suicide. Analysis is stymied by the force of the death wish, which becomes clearer as the search in depth proceeds . . .

At least the analyst sets out to make a personal relationship, and by no other bridge than a person who cares can the detached sufferer return to the fold of humanity from his cool, beat, outsiderish position. How useless drugs or physical treatments are bound to be is evident from the nature of the case.

Frankly, no psychiatric attempt can be made in the time allowed to change radically the withdrawn, detached personality, partly because our whole impersonal attitude as organically-minded psychiatrists is itself liable to be an expression of defence against a schizoid position in ourselves. I recognize a good deal of this in myself – and it is only the steady pressure of a warmly human wife and the exigencies of Christian living and thinking that have driven me to recognize how incapacitated for commitment I am on certain levels . . .

This is an agonizing contradiction, that one longs to trust but dare not, longs to die but dare not, lest perchance the death dream – and there's the rub – prolong the agony into a further eternity. How can it be resolved?

FL then invokes his text and Christ's call first to fellowship, then to the endurance of his absence, then to his coming again:

The first steps are the call and friendship of Christ, not as for the first disciples of the Lord in person, but of some Christian person or persons in whom he lives by his abiding Holy Spirit. This person should be characterized, not by intellectual reflectiveness and the capacity to give advice, but by the immediacy of spirit, a simple directness of apprehension of the reality of God, and the willingness to live obediently to his beck and call in being available to others. Unnoticed on your own stair there may be a withdrawn sufferer, one of the truly afflicted. Are you always gadding about with your own gang of friends? Could God get through to you to lead you to offer this kind of friendship to him?

... From living in college in another place recently, I am convinced that it is Christian students who are in fact doing most of the therapy that is being done – on this caring, personal level – for the overtly afflicted students who constitute at least ten per cent of the population in these places.

This caring induces the detached sufferer to come, however tentatively, out of his shell. He discovers, perhaps for the first time, a quality of non-oppressive concern that is a totally new factor in his experience. He may, and will if he is wisely guided, come to rely not only on friendship but on the objective means of God's personal self-giving. Without the former plethora of introspection as to its immediate effects on himself, he attends to God's portrayal of his face in Christ in Word and Sacrament. He still has no faith in any power of faith or commitment to be discovered in himself by an inward search. He has no need of it now. He sees Jesus objectively as the author and perfecter of his faith in God ... Though he cannot yet be related to his own abyss of non-being by direct introspection, he can be related to it, and in a sense accept it, through faith in Christ who is the 'harrower of Hell' for all men ...

The next stage is very painful:

Then, says Jesus, for a while you will see me no more ... The detached person has come to rely heavily on his Christian friends ... He often manifests an almost hysterical, clinging attachment to [them] ... This, unless overcome by an accession of spiritual courage, leads to an unhealthy, fanatical idealization of some person or to rigid adherence to an over-defined religious practice or cultic orthodoxy.

. . . To insist on temporal support is to behave as though the Eternal himself is incompetent. It is to stop half-way along the road to Christ's cure. It is to be content with the preliminary consolations, whereas the purpose of them, in the mind of the Divine Surgeon, was simply to strengthen the patient for the operation in depth that really effects a cure . . .

Here FL speaks of

. . . deliberately sinking down into your own agonizing nothingness, remembering the words of the Lord: Except a corn of wheat fall into the ground and die, it abideth alone.

He speaks of a minister who,

. . . fortified by a week's meditation on the fact of Christ's dereliction, was able to endure in consciousness the full experience of dread, in such a way as for ever to put it behind him. That which, in terms of agony, cost the Son of God most, namely God-forsakenness, is the only valid therapeutic agent for the ultimate agony of the human spirit.

In this dark night of the soul there is no help from the temporal, either persons or mental pictures. In this cloud of unknowing the soul is pressed nakedly upon the truth and being of God . . . This is the completion in depth of your baptism. Again you go under the waters and actually, in a strong spiritual sense, die under them.

Then follows the final stage of God's cure of the afflicted person: 'Again a little while and ye shall see me.' Christ's baptism of pain and dereliction and death accomplished, he rose to fullness of life and said, 'Because I live ye shall live also.'

At the end of these stages, his whole outlook is changed:

If the exigencies of affliction have driven a man along this road to the place where nothing but the Eternal can relieve his suffering, and the Eternal Son does, in the final analysis, enable him so to endure as to transcend his pain for ever, he is not inclined to ask any more academic questions about the problem of evil. Without his own share of innocent affliction he would never have been impelled so desperately to wrestle with God for a revelation of his nature or the vision of his face.

Seventeen years after this sermon was delivered, FL wrote about his 'new and more adequate understanding of the origins of "affliction" ' in the magazine *Energy and Character*.[12] As we saw in Chapter 3, the concept of 'Maternal-Foetal Distress' involved a new perception of the origins of mental pain, and a new approach to dealing with it, but Christ remained the therapist:

It has always been recognized by psychotherapy, and indeed by pastoral care, that we should aim to get at the roots of any personality disorder. The eradication of any deep trouble depends, by definition, on our reaching the primal or original source of it. What we are being led to realize is that the tap-roots of affliction go much deeper into our personal history than even birth itself. This may surprise and even offend us. There are obstacles in the way of our even considering the evidence, if we have for years given our professional seal to dynamic interpretations of much later origin.

However, this evidence is now available. And with it comes a new dimension to St Paul's Letter to the Ephesians. We are part of those 'ages to come', in which the 'not yet searched out' riches of the redemptive down-reach of Christ will be revealed. We see this as part of the mysterious plan by which God has promised to reconcile our humanity to his creative purpose, in spite of all its persistent tendency to miscarry. To put right the miscarriages of justice that go on in foetal life will not only re-root our humanity. It will shake the principalities and powers that may rely for their persuasiveness on the distrust and unbelief that we collected in the placental letter box.

Wherever the point of origin is found to be, the following still holds true:[13]

. . . Our wider evangelism in the secular world must be prepared to meet the resistances that come from the hystero-schizoid position and the death of god images in the abyss of dread. To such people the approach by way of moralism, of the categorical imperative, of 'you ought', 'you are responsible to God's law', 'you are guilty of transgression', this approach which makes good inner sense to the personalities of those who are prone to depression, or obsessional reactions, rings absolutely no bells at all with those in whom 'the dreadful has already happened'. I do not even believe that the Holy Spirit means them to be approached in this way.

There is no valid proclamation of the gospel to them except in the preaching of the Cross. Even in this we do not emphasize it so much as the place where sins against the moral law are forgiven, as the place where God himself is identified with the innocent bearing of cataclysmic evil. Both the evils we have suffered and the evils we have committed are dealt with on the Cross. It is characteristic of the depressed theologian that he is prone to an over-emphasis of the morality, guilt, sin, forgiveness dimension, at the expense of that which makes most sense to the afflicted. They need first to be assured about the nature of God, and to be convinced that he knows what kind of world it is that he has thrown them into. The demonic powers are much closer to the surface in the Gentile world than they are in the solidarities of Judaism, or indeed of that combination of Roman and Jewish we have so largely inherited in our Churches. To the Gentile world we must preach Christ's victory over the demonic powers, which means again the evangelization of the unconscious dread . . .

Reviewing his earlier teaching about hystero-schizoid dynamics in the light of his later findings on maternal-foetal distress, this is what he said in seminars in 1981.[14] (It is clear that, as he speaks, he is illustrating his words with the hystero-schizoid chart used in the seminars. Figures are shown crawling out of the abyss in the directions of attachment to people, on the one side, and detachment from them, to the point of ivory tower seclusion, on the other.)

Here, fortunately, one doesn't need to make any major corrections, but just to say that this central place of dread occurs very early, and earlier than we used to think. Now, some people, having fallen into that abyss, crawl out of it in the direction of people . . . Others, who tend, perhaps, to have a higher intelligence, and tend to be rather more ectomorphic people, with more skin and nervous tissue, they are going to *think* their way through problems. Thus a division happens. Not a total division, because there is always some schizoid in the hysteric, and always some hysteric in the schizoid. But in general, these two patterns of response are now open to a person. And this is the basis of our understanding of hysteria, and the basis of our understanding of the schizoid position. And you see that they are mirror images of each other. The hysterical person feels horribly detached, and is crawling up here to compel someone . . . 'to attach themselves to me or I'll attach myself to them.' Whereas the schizoid person says, 'Never again, thank you. Not human beings, not after what they've done.' And so you get this building of the ivory tower in the mind, and living by detachment.

The hysterical person's question is, 'Will they like me?' The schizoid person says, 'Will they leave me alone?'

5

The Defence of the Personality – Part II

THE PARANOID REACTION PATTERN

On the Dynamic Cycle, paranoid reactions are shown to be a response, not to grave suffering at birth, nor to the absence or long delay in coming of the nurturing person, but to what are, or seem to be, persistent shortages of real nourishment or genuinely loving attention in the early stages of life. There has been enough acceptance to provide the infant with a strong sense of 'being' but it feels perennially short-changed, on short commons, given less than its due. There is no real sense of 'well-being'.

In his introduction to the teaching pamphlet *Clinical Pastoral Care in Paranoid States and Related Conditions*,[1] Frank Lake writes:

This is a group of intractable conditions, resistant to medical and psychiatric treatment. They tend to creep up on us insidiously in middle life, sapping away the strength of the whole personality just at the time when the mind and the body are entering into a slow decline from natural causes. To the inevitable attenuation of our vitalities is added, from the long-lost wasteland of infancy, a fearful memory of earlier wanderings in dry places. Since these memories were repressed even as they occurred, they have been a lifelong constituent of the personality.

. . . Under stress of contemporary failure of the resources of well-being, the hidden persecutoriness of life has had to be projected on to other people who are 'getting at us', or on to our own body, which is 'letting us down'. Our behaviour becomes paranoid, or fixed in hypochondriacal self-concern. At times, the roots of wretchedness emerge in their entirety in states of exhaustion and 'unwarranted' fatigue . . .

It is not only when things are going ill with us that these intolerable slow diminishments are forced upon our awareness.

Abundant health may press them to the surface like a foreign body. The action of the Holy Spirit must open up the empty places if they are to be filled, disclosing what we are needlessly ashamed of . . .

In the first printing of the pamphlet, he had used the case of a clergyman to illustrate this condition, creating a notion which he tries to dispel in the Second Impression:[2]

. . . Paranoid personalities are to be found just as commonly among doctors and politicians, civil servants and shop stewards. I come upon paranoid reactions in myself under certain kinds of stress. The more faithful we are to biblical priorities, the more ready we are to insist that judgement begins at the household of God. I began . . . not with judgement but with diagnosis. My friends do me a kindness when they help me to recognize and withdraw my projections, to stop defending by denial against the weakness that is my own. How else shall Christ become our physician?

Since, to the paranoid personality, nothing that happens has ever seemed to be his or her own fault, but always due to the malignity, stupidity, or neglect of others, such people seldom ask for, or take kindly to, counselling:

. . . Some [seminar members] have asked, 'Can you ever communicate the specifically Christological resources you have mentioned meaningfully to paranoid sufferers?' Seldom, directly. Christ was identified on the Cross with the specific forms of suffering which they have suffered, but are now denying vehemently. They could not admit his relevance without declaring their inner feelings of disgrace. This they cannot do. But those who are drawn into their orbit to 'help' . . . are often so dragged down and humiliated by destructive accusations of uselessness that it is they who first can see and accept, with deep feeling, the resources of Christ's own fortitude. They accept this as he did, and Paul came to do, within a weakness that is as humiliating and crushing as it is unjust.

In fact, as we saw in the first chapter (p. 2), FL considered 'the Spirit of Life in Christ Jesus' as the only resource likely to be effective in helping paranoid sufferers to accept their own inner truth.

In Finland, in 1978, FL had been asked by a group called the Free Evangelical Association to speak, he says, 'not as a psychiatrist . . . about how to receive the Holy Spirit in counselling'. In the tapes of these sessions, he talks about inner weakness, in various contexts and without clinical tags, as one aspect of personality:[3]

Denial of weakness. . . . Human character at its most religious best is a systematic telling of lies, because every man has got weakness inside him . . . *If you are a man you must deny your weakness.* The most successful man is the man who dramatizes his lies most successfully.

You've got this in the character of Peter. You remember how he dramatized himself: 'Lord, all men will betray you, but not me.' And so, in his mercy, Jesus had to take him to the Cross where he denied him. Peter could not become the head of the disciples or the leader of the Church until he learned about the lies in his own nature.

The further St Paul went on in his Christian life, the more there came up from inside him deep humiliations and deep weakness. People who have a lot of weakness and humiliation inside them very often have to become very important outside there. They persecute in other people the weakness they cannot face in themselves. So Paul, first of all, was a persecutor. But then, later on in life, he felt persecuted by his own weakness, and the Holy Spirit had to say, 'Paul, stay with your weakness. I'd like that to stay with you to remind you to the end of your days that you spent some of your earlier years as a very successful liar. When the High Priest sent you with letters to persecute the Christians, you said, "What a strong man I am! I will persecute these weak people. They humiliate our nation and we will humiliate them." Lies, lies and more lies.'

And so, when Paul met Christ on the Damascus road, the Lord said to him, 'Paul, you're persecuting me.' And, at the end of his days, Paul knew that the persecuted weakness inside him was being shared by the Christ he had persecuted.

Our need of others . . . Jesus needed friends. He needed people to be with him in his trouble and wasn't ashamed to ask, . . . as most religious people are. Most of us are ashamed to admit that we need friends to go into the trouble with us. But . . . the revival of the Church will never come until Christians admit that they need one another.

Difficulty of staying with weakness . . . Of our own human strength we never want to go into weakness, we avoid like anything the bloody sweat of our own Gethsemane. If people treat us unjustly we complain and are full of bitterness and resentment. We can stand a lot of things but we can't stand mocking . . . And when people are going through Gethsemane it looks rather disgusting. The natural man says, *I don't want to see this bloody sweat.* The natural man doesn't want to stay near groaning of this kind. It is very difficult to see, when somebody is going into this place of groaning and Gethsemane, that this is actually for the glory of God.

Only the Holy Spirit makes it possible . . . every variety of power, weakness, every variety of being loved or being hated, including crucifixion and resurrection, including the giving of love to friends and the happiness of meeting friends and finding them, the whole of our humanity is explored in depth by the power of the Holy Spirit.

> Expounding on the text of 2 Cor. 3:17 'Now the Lord is the Spirit and where the Spirit of the Lord is, there is freedom', he says:

Meeting Christ with unveiled faces. You've seen quite a lot of people among us here who you thought were perfectly happy persons . . . They had a good straight face with no problems. And then, the veil has been taken away and the tears have begun to flow. And then you begin to realize why Jesus had to go on the Cross and why he had to weep over Jerusalem. Civilization is about keeping your face veiled. It is about dramatizing yourself so that you can tell skilful lies. So that, as long as we are all veiled from one another, nobody will be troubled . . . But if you keep your eyes on Christ's face, and keep it unveiled, you are . . . ready to see the suffering person in others . . .

> Latterly FL became certain that paranoid feelings had their origin in the womb:[4]

. . . [The paranoid reaction pattern] is a character defence against primal loss of well-being, or humiliating weakness and emptiness, by denial and projection . . . The baby [*according to his earlier teaching*] felt identified with weak-being, with emptiness and meaninglessness, with a fearful sense of inferiority and low self-esteem. Well, with absolutely no alteration, you can take that into the first trimester . . . The truth . . . of the inward parts is now . . . uncertainties of supply [through the placenta]: *I'm denied well-being; I'm identified with weak-being and a nasty awareness of deficiency, forced to feel inferior.* His rights are denied, he's under-valued, worthless, self-esteem very low, status as a person low, achievement limited, feels useless . . . humiliated . . . dejected . . . [etc] And I assure you all that is intra-uterine, every single bit of it. We've had it in hundreds and hundreds of people.

Now, you see, if you retain that as your basic mode of experi-ence, you grow up to be an inadequate personality, with a deep sense that *I am no good, nothing ever goes well for me,* with hypochondriacal symptoms to boot. But the paranoid person is one who has had an experience of glory. And what they are protesting against is the come-down. Now . . . we never knew where the glory came from. But it would seem that, in some cases at least, in the paranoid personality, there is an awareness of the transcendent glory of the blastocystic phase — and indeed of any other good phase there has ever been, where *my rights were being maintained as they should be, by law.* Now the pain of this humiliation is so appalling that the defence against it is denial: I'm *never* uncertain, I am *not* weak, I lack *nothing.* I am *not* inferior, I am *not* poor, worthless, valueless, puny, useless. I'm *fine,* thank you.

Earlier in the same seminars, he had expressed it this way:[5]

With the paranoid person . . . where a person feels that *Somebody is influencing me, somebody knows my thoughts, they've got inside me, they're making me do things* — where people are not taking responsi-bility for their own boundaries and their own margins, but are experiencing a group, or their relationship as *It just takes all the energy out of me, I can't stop it.* Or *It just makes me angry,* and they can't give any good reason for it, then they are probably talking about the stuff that has its origin down here [*I presume, pointing to his navel*], where . . . things do happen that you can't protect yourself from.

ANXIETY

The title FL gave to his teaching pamphlet on this subject, *Clinical Pastoral Care in States of Overt Anxiety and of Conditions in which, though Latent, Fixated Threats to Being-itself are Mani-fested in the Form of Phobic Reactions, Autonomic Reactions, Disso-ciative Reactions, Depersonalization and Conversion Reactions,* will make it clear why we can only touch on it here. This comes from his introduction:

The study of anxiety can be made easy only by falsifying it. We cannot 'go into' it without being disturbed by it. Its origins in us are lost in obscurity. Its roots reach down to primitive experiences such as birth itself and the vulnerability of babyhood. For our adult modes of experience we have a vocabulary which is generally understood, but for these shadowy threats we lack a precise language. What we say can seldom be validated scientifically. Every 'ology' concerning man has a language of its own which attempts to comprehend anxiety. Until we have taken into consideration all that human beings regard as 'terribly' or 'dreadfully' important to them, we have not fully comprehended anxiety. To discover the right hypotheses, the ultimately valid language, the proper interpretive word from a man in dread for the dread that holds all men in bondage, is our real therapeutic quest.

Anxiety resists our attempts to capture and control it by the intellect, pure science, or rationality. It is irrational. It transcends all the categories in which, for our professional convenience, we would like to confine it. It transcends the basic division between sickness and health. It can be the most constructive force in creative characters; yet nothing is more destructive in those whose power of being cannot contain it. Anxiety is a central concern for existentialist philosophy and ontology, but equally so for the biochemist occupied with the physiology and pharmacology of stress in the bodily organism. The focus of anxiety may be on what happened before breathing commenced, or on what may happen when breathing is again becoming difficult in the moment of death, or even on the hereafter . . .

Pastoral care can define its own proper task in relation to anxiety only when those who undertake it are aware of the ways in which it is drawn into the conceptual framework and practice of other disciplines. It does not do to know only one language and one remedy in relation to anxiety. Enthusiasts, carelessly blind to other approaches, will set out to treat the anxieties of others unaware of the extent to which they are covertly treating their own. If we do this, we forfeit the right to make a critical appraisal of other approaches, which at this stage is most necessary. So do persevere: to be able to bear the anxiety of studying anxiety here in print, may be a prelude to encountering it more directly in oneself and in others. Ultimately we may be able to include all its negations in our total affirmation of life through the Cross and Resurrection of Christ.

That the most terrible social welfare cases, like those involving child abuse or neglect, are sometimes, somehow, inexplicably overlooked or neglected by social workers must be apparent to any newspaper reader. Has it anything to do with the intolerable anxiety such cases raise even in well-trained and conscientious professionals? FL undoubtedly thought so, for the subject he chose for a lecture to The Conference of Social Workers, in Bristol in 1965, was called 'Education for Tolerance'.[6] In it he said:

Every intolerable situation begins as a tolerable one, a bearable stress which eventually rises to a crisis and passes beyond the threshold into that which is overwhelming. This progression takes place whether the subject of stress is an experimental animal, as in Pavlov's experiments, a client, a caseworker, a family, or society itself. Education for tolerance must, among other things, mean 'drawing out of' other people inherent powers of tolerance. It means helping them to suffer more without becoming overwhelmed, enabling them to endure more frustration with fewer signs and symptoms of intolerance. Even if we are talking about the desirability that people in general should become more tolerant of those who suffer from neurosis, we recognize that their intolerance is the projection of aspects of their own personalities which they cannot yet tolerate in consciousness. We shall only make them more tolerant under stress by enabling them to see more, accept more, and to bear more of their own fixated infantile experiences of injuries to trust, which were so intolerable as to be split off from the remaining ego.

. . . Casework training could be described simply as a . . . training in tolerating the anxieties generated in all of us by close contact with people who find life unbearable. Anxiety is infectious . . .

And courage is needed to deal with it:[7]

The need for superhuman tolerance of distressed people arises at the point where their anxieties begin to reverberate and resonate in the deep areas of our own unconscious negativities. Much the same ultra-maximal stress and painful splitting lies buried, under a now less adequate covering of repression, in our own minds. Our skill alone cannot now function without our courage. The form of the courage required here, as Tillich suggests, is twofold. The courage to be as oneself, alone, in spite of separation anxiety, is demanded as you leave the safe world of uncomprehending but confident people to descend to where the client may be found. That is the first necessity. The second aspect of courage is the courage to be as part of another person, identified with him, in spite of commitment anxiety, though the world has written him off and the scorn of the proud writes us off because our association contaminates us in their eyes.

This is certainly where I find my own nature stretched, almost beyond endurance at times. . . . I badly want to get away, to escape to a safer, saner world. But my patient's power to bear what he has to endure in the abreaction, to bear the threat of non-being in a power of being that can absorb the pain and thus overcome it for ever, depends on my staying with him.

> Rather diffidently, since the members of his audience are not necessarily Christians, FL suggests a source of strength that makes this possible:[8]

Though of course what I say now carries no proof of cause and effect, I share the conviction of other Christians that . . . Christ, being now alive, can work in us his own wide tolerance of these . . . anxieties. He does this whenever, in following him, our turn comes to bear, or share, the mental pain of others. I have at times come to the end of what is, for me, tolerable. But that does not necessarily mean backing out, but rather restructuring the therapeutic situation so as to relate myself primarily to Christ and his promised resources of courage for both of us. . . . No particular subjective experience follows this reorientation; simply an access of power to go on bearing, with a sense of being steadied, if not carried, myself.

In a long article on 'The care of the anxious',[9] FL describes anxiety as:

. . . protean in its manifestation, a symptom of fearful complexity. No profession as yet exists which takes up all the determinants and links of anxiety, from the genetic to the spiritual, with equal seriousness.

And also:[10]

Anxiety is a troublesome subject nowadays, since its incidence is probably mounting and no one of the helping professions is particularly eager to care for the anxious . . . What is anxiety, anyway? Why do some patients respond gratifyingly to drugs, and others, 50 per cent of them apparently, discard the pills the psychiatrist has ordered, as if they had been expecting something other than pills? When is it proper to repress anxiety at all costs, and when is it better to discuss its origins and ramifications as deeply as time permits?

> This being so, it is good to find him responding to a letter in *Renewal* magazine with the kind of straightforward, sympathetic advice that many people similarly afflicted might take to heart. First the question:[11]

Dear Dr Lake

I am an anxious person. At times I feel at peace but all sorts of situations bring back sensations of panic, with vague fears of some impending disaster. I have prayed for healing. My friends have prayed. Why doesn't it happen?

I want to serve God, but how can I be a full Christian and give a clear witness to his power while this continues? Am I letting God down? Or, and I hardly like to ask this question, 'Is God not answering because I am worthless?' I certainly feel worthless, and useless to the friends whose advice doesn't work for me. They despair of me and I am a burden to myself. What can I do?

> FL begins by saying that it is unsatisfactory to be counselling 'via the column', and then, as in his earlier article on anger, by restating the problem in such a way as to give his enquirer fresh insight into it. He then continues:

. . . your desire to trust people and be lovingly dependent on them is, perhaps, cross-matched with so much experience of rejection, or of merely conditional acceptance, that you are driving, at the same time, in the opposite direction, towards a defensive independence. I think it is always the case that those who suffer from chronic, severe anxiety are locked in an internal contradiction of this kind. To relieve their anxieties, they would have to rush in this direction and the opposite direction simultaneously.

It may be, on the other hand, that your anxiety emerges from a phase in your life when the Father himself is bringing you into contact with your insecure beginnings, in what could be wholly creative ways, though it doesn't *feel* like that at the moment . . . As the peace of God presses down into the deepest recesses of our being, fear and apprehension gain strength to make their appearance in consciousness. So far so good. The trouble starts when, in all honesty, you attempt to share this emerging pain with your fellow Christians. They cannot take it . . . Religious people shy away from those who cannot cover up, or do not wish to cover up, genuinely painful feelings . . . And if they do get through to advising you, the would-be helpers may even use the Lord's own words, 'Do not be anxious. Your Heavenly Father knows what you need.' You try to put this into practice, but it . . . doesn't work.

This is not because the advice is wrong, untrue or unscriptural. Obviously not. The futility of it derives from the emotional climate in which the advice is given . . . You feel that your friends . . . are implicitly or actually critical of your wavering faith. Their looks, if not their speech, indicate that you are a poor example . . . I would like you to look at the climate in which you are being asked to change.

He then uses two parables to illustrate the kind of emotional climate necessary if we are to change. In doing this, he is not only responding to the questioner but suggesting to all readers of the magazine what a Christian group can be for its members:

. . . The climate of God's love for us in Christ means that we are never put down but always lifted up, never put out into the cold, but always brought into the warmth. As Mother Julian of Norwich used to say, if we are cluttered about with feelings of blame, this is our problem, not God's, for he has declared us blameless in Christ . . .

The Prodigal Son was not asked to change his clothes in the pigsty among people who despised him. This was asked of him only when he was already at home, in the warm atmosphere of his father's never-interrupted acceptance and care. His transformation would begin, so to speak, with a bath in front of the kitchen fire. As the old rags that smelt of pigs were being thrown to the back of the fire, the new clothes are already hanging over a chair, aired and warm. The father is there, delighting in his son, half the grown man he is, half the child he used to be and needs to be again. The servants all reflect the father's 'unconditional positive regard'.[12] They fully accept the wanderer who such a short time ago believed himself to be utterly unacceptable. The door is shut on the cold draught of the elder brother's criticism. This is the climate most of us need if a total, 'down to the skin' change of inner and outer personality clothing is taking place.

I remember coming into a warm welcoming house out of sleet and an icy wind at the end of a 30-mile trek, all of it over 10,000 feet up in the Himalayas. Sitting in front of the fire, drinking countless cups of hot tea, I began to thaw out and to shiver uncontrollably, as I had not been doing whilst still out in the cold. It is like that when an anxious person, who has been controlling the feelings of panic, comes into the relaxed, all-accepting, be-what-you-are hospitality of the body of Christ. You don't know how cold you were until you come into the warmth, how anxious you were until you come into the peace. This peace passes all human understanding because it isn't in the least bit threatened or diminished by your giving way for the pent-up anxiety to express itself fully. It welcomes you as you are. This is the gospel. The other puts you somehow under a law, a law which Christ has killed and done away with.

He gives the anxious reader firm counsel:

So you can choose, and we always have some choice in this matter, to breathe deeply and broadly, and to let your mind wander in the green pastures with the good shepherd, or, like the prodigal, round the warm, well-furnished rooms of your Father's house. Just simply decline to let the fretful child in you rule your life . . . If you discover yourself being dominated by the inner child, you will notice that its breathing is so shallow and irregular as to be a perfect recipe for the very anxiety it is complaining about. You can choose to breathe deeply, both in the sense of natural air around you and the spiritual air provided by the Holy Spirit, who is the breath of God . . .

God's peace does not exclude these most anxiety-provoking human situations, the more terrible when they happen to us in infancy and reverberate through from those depths. The peace of God is inclusive of everything that has ever happened to human beings which could disqualify God's goodness or justify us when, like Job, we accuse him as innocent sufferers.

He ends by saying that he hopes his advice will not be felt as yet a further burden:

If I have enabled you to move into this true climate of your Father's love, to that extent you will already be able to bear your anxieties in a new way, with your faith in him, and in yourself as always his, strengthened, not weakened. If I have not been able to do this, can you let the failure be mine?

Remarks made to members of the Post Green seminars underline his instructions about breathing. Breathlessness can be both the cause and the result of our anxiety:[13]

. . . civilization is the disease of not breathing . . . We have discovered, as [Fritz] Perls said, that 'anxiety is excitation without oxygen'. We try . . . not to breathe, not to feel again the awful things that go on in our gut. And . . . breathing again, of course, does challenge you with the presence of this stuff, and if you have the power to integrate it, and go on breathing, you go on being more and more alive . . . But on the whole [not breathing] is the choice, which diminishes the oxygen input, which limits your sensitivity again. And this is a way of blocking the [hurtful] stuff. You see? . . . one has got to use tranquillizers sometimes, because the amount of anxiety is more than a person can cope with . . . Something that diminishes the oxygen input, and therefore diminishes the amount of pain, is something that human nature has wanted from time immemorial.

6

Clinical Theology and Other Therapies

Readers may wonder how Clinical Theology relates to other forms or styles of therapy with which they are familiar. It is clearly not an entity apart. Everything Frank Lake wrote shows that he was an avid reader, well informed of developments in his field and always on the lookout for new ideas and methods of working with people that could be incorporated into his own theoretical framework, so as to enlarge and deepen the skills and understanding of counsellors in training. He summed up his attitude thus:[1]

Each of the major successful methods of therapy and counselling . . . has begun with a germ of genius, a sudden discovery of a new way of seeing. This has led to an economical and coherent simplification that had been overlooked by others. Each has developed a training programme, an organization, international outreach, and has accredited representatives to operate in its name.

Those of us who came to these therapies in our early days were introduced to their most productive ideas, and have learned to use them discriminately. Our task is to keep close to the client, as Rogerian,[2] or Truax and Carkhuff[3] counselling training has taught us to do. Often, when we are unsure as to how to proceed in helping a client, one or other of these methods clicks into focus, and we can offer it as a way of working and understanding.

But I have no loyalty to any one of these particular methods, and I have no wish to stretch its applicability to cover the whole range of human problems. *Eclecticism is the correct theological stance.* I am grateful to them all, particularly for what they have written so clearly.

He felt a strong affinity with many therapists who did not

share his Christian faith. Under the heading 'Are some humanists more realistic about man's concrete dilemma than the classical theologians?' he wrote:[4]

It falls to me to work in close fellowship with humanists, psycho-therapists, those particularly who practise in Gestalt Therapy, Transactional Analysis, Bioenergetics, Primal Therapy or Peri-natal Integration[5] – in which events before, during, and after birth are vividly relived. Most of these movements were founded by Jewish refugees from Hitler's regime. There is a Hebrew and biblical quality to their understanding of man which is closer to the New Testament than the classic Platonism or Aristotelianism in which our theological schools are nurtured. As I work with these men, facing together the concrete problems of helping human beings to grow out of their fears, wretchedness and alien-ation into a more abundant life, we understand each other thoroughly in the secular language that we use. We can ask ultimate questions about man in this language . . . Our 'the-ology' by definition must be inductive. It must be relevant to the discernible problems of existence . . .

In an interview in *Self and Society*,[6] he was asked the ques-tion, 'What have you felt about working in the Humanistic Psychology movement during the last couple of years?' To which he replied:

I have been very moved that all the old barriers that seemed to exist because we were projecting all kind of bad things onto each other are beginning to go. Those of us who maintain, or have come to, a religious background can recognize that the 'God' they don't believe in, we don't believe in either . . . If people are hoping that 'God's' help would be of the kind which he gives to the immature, to take them off the hook and make it all easier, well, that may be a preliminary in our spiritual, psychological or therapeutic journey. But ultimately, our mature selves know that our real problem is to find a 'God' who will help us 'to get our noses to the grindstone' (that's a nice metaphor!), to help us bear that which human nature all too often shrinks from. A living Truth to stop our human nature . . . running away from the reality of the depths of us, which we are trained to believe is too painful to bear. I think we agree here . . .

When his interlocutor said that what they shared most was a faith in the process, he agreed.

Yes, a faith in facing honestly a process which commonsense and our ordinary humanity warn us to run away from. And yet our integrity knows that if we do, we lose something more precious than this time-bound life . . . As we join in caring groups, to grasp our deepest, most painful and most joyful experiences, our hearts are opened, our desires known and secrets are shared . . . When this is the process, truth and reality are born and tested in our hearts.

In the same year, 1978, the editorial board of *Contact*, of which he was a member, invited him to be guest editor of an issue devoted to 'The Newer Therapies'.[7] His own long article, plus three others which he commissioned,[8] show both what he valued and what he found wanting in some of the therapies that had come to the fore in the sixties and seventies. Almost without knowing it, anyone working with him, or taking part in CT seminars, was absorbing a wide variety of ideas, gleaned from many different sources, for assessing what is going on in troubled people and helping them to feel better. His increasing concern, however, was with more radical change:

The newer therapy most closely identified with CTA is a continuation of our psychotherapeutic practice since 1954 in assisting patients to come into direct contact with the very earliest experiences of life that were sufficiently painful, weakening, distressing or frightening as to require splitting off from consciousness and repression . . . We have always been aware that Freud and Rank referred to these layers of experience as 'Primal'. In this sense my psychiatric colleagues and I were [already] doing what is now, by Janov and his associates, called Primal Therapy[9] in the 50s and through the 60s. We would not wish to claim that we do Primal Therapy as Janov's Institute does it. We have our own way to the reliving and reconnecting of primal events. [*See Chapter 3, under 'Maternal-Foetal Distress'. Ed.*]

Introducing the commissioned articles on 'Re-evaluation Counselling' (or 'Co-counselling') and 'Prayer Counselling' ('Victorious Ministry'), he writes:

I regard these two lay therapies as too significant and important to leave out. The one is secular but, like Transactional Analysis, Gestalt and Bioenergetics, is so humanly and biblically sound in principle (i.e. of mutual aid between ordinary people in discharging painful and blocked emotions) that it can be Christened, with great gain in liveliness, sharing, reality and humanness, in the churches. The other is too deeply and radically Christian in its expectations of the Spirit's transforming power at depth to be credible, yet, to most churchgoers . . . or academic theologians . . . But respect and awareness are growing.

It is a striking confirmation of a new fact in our age that both a secular development, *Primal Integration*, and the Spirit-led *Prayer Counselling* speak with one voice: *Traumatic perinatal events are eminently recoverable, and with great benefit.*

FL goes on to discuss the uneasy relationships between secular and Christian humanism:

. . . We in CTA hope to exercise the bridging function that first prompted our existence . . . an attempt to bridge the river that ran between secular psychiatry and Christian theology, not so much at the intellectual headwaters as down towards the estuary where thousands come to one bank or the other, hopefully, to drink some healing waters. So mutually negligent were these two of each other's existence, you might have said it was the River Styx, the toxic boundary river of the Underworld, that ran between them. In our professional lives we still mostly walk apart, well warned not to linger on the banks, lest the scientific psychiatrist be seen tainted with religious enthusiasm or the priest/minister be dubbed an amateur psychiatrist. Yet if there is any good to be gained from either of us, our beneficiaries are compelled *by our arrangements* to spend time walking backwards and forwards on the bridge between us . . .

As for my own science, enshrined in the Royal College of Psychiatrists and in the pages of its Journal, I am puzzled as I look on the multitudes who come down in their very human predicaments to our side of the river for understanding and relief. There is a thick mist on the meadows, a dense fog in places.

What is this cloud? A gracious haze, covering with partial oblivion senses made raw by too much painful tension, or a thick fog of undiscriminating tranquilliser, a miasma of dulled sensibility and conditioned mediocrity. The prescription of an antidepressant or anxiolytic drug has given to many of us a measure of relief from apparently meaningless mental pain for a while. These, too, are 'newer therapies', for which the demand is insistent and the expense immense.

He describes this conflict between psychiatry and religion as one which can only be overcome through an intellectual, moral or religious conversion. Then, from the subject of tranquillizers, he goes on to talk about bad and good pain:

. . . Usually we think of healing as the abolition of the common enemy, some presumably pointless pain (though one of the first things the medical student learns is not to risk letting an inflamed appendix perforate by masking the pain with a pain-killer). But we also consider it to be a form of healing when we take part in a wider-ranging process in which the person to be healed, in the pursuit of what they . . . judge to be a greater good, makes a decision, or takes a stand, which actually involves them in bearing more pain . . . It seems that the immediate relief of pain could only have been accepted by forfeiting the gain which was coming from taking the longer view. So it is a choice between one level of pain and another. The pain of a 'cross' freely taken up and truly borne for love, or even duty, or responsibility, or identification with another, can be a good pain which no wise person would lightly surrender.

I am not here concerned to argue any position as my own, because I find myself on either side of this divide on different occasions. I want to insist that the newer therapies, in helping people to take responsibility to bear, and so assimilate more of, their shut-away childhood and adult pain, are taking up an authentic dialectical position which has been in danger of going by default. Neither psychiatrists of the organic school (tranquillizers t.d.s.) nor ministers of religion (tranquillizer once a Sunday – if that is not too unkind to their congregations' typical response to even their most rousing sermons) have spent the hours required to enable their charges *to discover the transforming inner uses of adversity by providing a well-led and supportive group within which, should the person so wish, productive pain could be intensified.*

Yet whenever that recapitulation of past hurts does happen, the gain in personal authenticity is always considerable. It was a great step forward in St Francis of Assisi's discipleship when he gained the courage to meet and hold, kiss and love, the leper outside himself. What I am asking we should take note of is an even greater enhancement of authenticity when a man or woman gains the needed courage, within a non-perturbable group, to meet and hold, welcome and identify with, the one who has always felt like a leper inside [his or her] self . . .

Yet later, referring, as he so often did, to Søren Kierke-gaard's painful struggles towards faith, he issues a warning:

. . . Nothing is more terrifying than this. Unless the essentially *un-mediated* uncertainty of solitary, primal dread can be recapitu-lated in later life with the close support of the human 'Body of Christ', so as to *mediate* the certainty of safe transit through the paroxysmal uncertainty of these crushing hells and solitary purgatories of babyhood, they should not be re-entered . . .

He ends this section of his article by saying categorically:

Since Fairbairn, Balint and Winnicott, among the most senior British analysts, it has been increasingly clear that the basic existential, theological and moral problems of contemporary human beings are lost in the mists of *pre-verbal* experiences. They long antedate the announcement of parent Laws, and the naughty breaking of them by a rebellious child who collects guilt thereby. Francis Mott, Nandor Fodor and Otto Rank[10] have recorded what devastation can be wrought *in utero* by murderous feelings and abortifacient acts on the part of the mother. And many of us have long experience of what birth can do to engender catastrophic fears, self-destructive rages and a host of feelings so unbearable as to have needed repression ever after.

The newer therapies have given notice that primal integration is not beyond the bounds of therapeutic possibility if the leader-ship commitment and group support is fully adequate. I am trying to put all this in the setting of a theological and soteriolog-ical dialectic. I hope that for some of you, 'your hearts will burn within you as we talk on the road', and that this will be for you an opening out towards the deeper reaches of the 'not yet searched out' riches of Christ, and that you wonder, with me, whether we have not Christ alongside us nowadays 'interpreting to us in all the Scriptures the things concerning himself'. Unless we are badly mistaken, these are some of the depth realities we need to know to commend him to our generation as he deserves to be commended.

His next section speaks of a shift of theological emphasis, in ministering to the distressed, from concern with righteousness of life to focusing on the personal life history:

This means that we focus on the life history, on the passage of the Christian's life through various crises and transitions parallel to Christ's own. Therefore, in pastoral care, too, we focus on spending time in listening to the unfolding life-saga of conflict and struggle, call and confirmation, dark night and bewilderment, on peaks of glory and descents into hell, on 'God' too close, in what feels like his wrath, and too far away, in what feels like his desertion. All this openness and eagerness to share the other person's life story is characteristic of the newer therapeutic group and growth therapies. They would, therefore, seem to be nearer to the New Testament pattern than the 'sin clinics' of the confessors or the 'sin examinations' of the Kirk Sessions of old. People feel themselves to be part of the Body of Christ, as the group shows a personal interest in their unique yet sharably-human life history . . .
    This is in marked contrast to religious meetings . . . which . . . try to send people home with the illusion that they are all alike and have all agreed . . .
    There is an accent, too, in the newer therapies, on improvisation, experimentation and inductive feeling, intuition, and thinking – that is, on activity which starts with a close faithfulness to *what is actually going on* in the people opening themselves to the group's concern . . . Always to the fore is what the person and the group together, waiting on God, *discover*.

Elements of Eric Berne's Transactional Analysis (TA)[11] and of Gestalt Therapy,[12] particularly its use of Fantasy Journeys and the Empty Chair, have become woven into the fabric of the Clinical Theology training programme. Gestalt methods, FL points out, are better experienced than described, and are hard to grasp from the printed page. On TA, however, he reflects 'both from the angle of other therapies – and theologically', making some important distinctions:

TA has shown itself a flexible adjunct to pastoral care and counselling . . . the most widespread and readily useful of the newer therapies . . . able to release ordinary people into a sense of competence in understanding how they can improve on the

103

ways they relate to one another, breaking down barriers and moving towards a proper intimacy and emotional contact in families and among friends.

It could hardly be so easily grasped if it had not, in parts, sacrificed depth and adequacy in comprehending man, for the sake of brevity and panache, to a certain superficiality, especially on the frontier with ultimate meanings and morals. Theology must guard those... In CT we have held to a Christian ontology, which affirms . . . that true human being is . . . 'a being in Christ' . . . It is to 'become a partaker of the divine nature' (2 Peter 1:4), to 'become a dwelling place for God in the Spirit' (Eph. 2:22) . . .

The humanistic 'I'm O.K., You're O.K.',[13] which is the basis of TA, is affirming that beyond the acceptance TA members give each other, reality itself supports all self-acceptance. If, for a while, I forget myself and reality and reject you, I am out of touch with reality. The TA scriptures do not leave enough room for a quarrel between my basic acceptance of myself and others as to being-itself and to our undergirding relationship, and my disapproval and rejection of any wicked or irresponsible behaviour we are objectively guilty of committing. It is all O.K. All is excused. As a result, a dialogue between the Adult and his conscience is switched onto the axis between the internal Parent and the Child . . . So the voice of an authentic conscience is commonly 'turned off'. It is dismissed as the restriction of a Parental 'witch message'.

About TA's over-readiness to put down Parental injunctions, several observations are necessary.

Firstly, to assert that every truly 'nurturing Parent' must indicate constraints and limits to the growing child. The product of lax parenting becomes a shapeless psychopath, socially inept and irresponsible . . .

Secondly, we affirm that the Communal Parent is the source, for every new generation, of the inherited wisdom of previous generations . . . There must be legitimated power in society to define what would make its life impossible, to ban certain offences and punish or restrain offenders. Compliance with the justice of this transgenerational Communal Parent occurs as part of Adult common sense . . .

Thirdly, the demotion of the voice of the valid conscience into that of the pig Parent, and the sleight of hand which causes culpable guilt to disappear into the thin air of neurotic guilt, is a serious shortcoming in TA viewed as a Christian pastoral resource . . .

Yet he has approving things to say:

Eric Berne's aphorism, 'People are born princes and princesses, until their parents turn them into frogs', holds out something of the same welcome to children as Christ did when, announcing the coming of God's Kingdom, he named the children its basic sons and daughters.

And also:

The approach of Jesus to publicans and sinners, who had been messed about by life, was precisely this same breath-taking 'I'm O.K., You're O.K.'. He received them as friends and sealed his friendship . . . by eating with them.

FL concludes, however:

TA has no message of eternal life in Christ. Only in places where being nice equals being Christian could it be mistaken for a Gospel substitute . . . It has its own deliverance ministry, mundane but magnificently simple . . . Berne . . . deemed ordinary people capable of understanding their own personality problems and, through TA, of taking the steps that would put both inner and outer relationships to rights.

PRIMAL INTEGRATION

The remainder of his article is devoted to the subject of primal integration. This was the therapy which preoccupied him above all else at this time. Funds had been raised to make it possible for CTA to grant him a sabbatical in the last four months of 1977. Shortly afterwards, in March 1978, he suffered a stroke. Though he recovered, it became obvious that he could not do all he had done before, and it was then decided that he should devote himself to his research in the primal field, while the work of the Association was carried on by others.

A lecture which he prepared on Arthur Janov, whose book *The Primal Scream* described one of the best-known 'newer therapies', became a launch-pad for FL's own most cherished theories:[14]

It is obvious that I would not be attempting this lecture unless I believed that Janov's primal therapy has important insights to offer us. It is equally plain that I do not agree with his assertion that his findings cannot be integrated into other therapies, because, in fact, I have integrated some of what I take to be his methods and insights into my own. His peremptory exclusiveness presents eclectic psychotherapists such as I have always been with quite insoluble problems . . .

I find Janov a most unreliable guide, full of misunderstanding, when he makes pronouncements about American religion, and imagines that he is defining the Christian faith and dismissing it, when what he is dealing in is simply religion and moralism . . . But, [despite] reservations against his claims to infallibility, I find many of the things he has written so true to my own experience, so admirably expressed and so important, indeed essential, to depth healing and radical reconciliation, that I want to share them with you and pay tribute to his genius. . . .

After taking issue with Janov on a few other points, he goes on:

Both Freud and the religious believe in the need for mental defences against buried pains, tribulations and afflictions. They are aware of potentially explosive internal memories which are assumed to be so disruptive of a person's ability to cope, if not actually destructive of sanity, that they must be kept in check by repression, dissociation, denial, and displacement, that is, by one or other of the mental defence mechanisms. . . .

Janov does not deny that these defences have a 'second-order' naturalness for domesticated human beings . . . 'Defences are necessary,' he writes (*The Primal Revolution*, p. 24) 'when we are young and fragile and cannot take too much assault.' The question is, do we need to keep them when we are adult? . . .

. . . Defences can be modified but not dispensed with – that is the message alike of classical psychoanalysis and of Rogerian counselling in its many forms and extensions into the pastoral psychology and clinical pastoral educational fields. It certainly is a fundamental tenet of religion. It would be the main claim to fame of psycho-pharmacology as practised by organically orientated psychiatrists; they can add so much thickness to the defensive blanket against primal happenings and their memory traces . . .

Janov writes (*PR*, p. 25) 'The most basic difference between the classical Freudian approach and the primal one is that the Freudians believed that the unconscious, or id, is basically destructive and maladaptive, and that defences are needed to hold it back and help us adapt to outside realities. We [the Primal people] believe that what is unconscious is *real* and healthy, and that defences against that reality are what make us unreal and maladapted. . . .' Reflecting theologically, I find myself agreeing with Janov's dual concept of an original right relatedness to the sources, and the subsequent fall out of relationship to them. . . .

To Janov (as to Reich, Lowen, and the bioenergetic therapists) the body is the precious repository of one's own personal history, particularly of its painful parts, the pleasurable parts having been assimilated and become part of the courage with which we meet life itself. In this view, our history of unbearable pain is so embedded in our bodies, that if there were to be any Saviour appointed for man, he would need, first and foremost, to reconcile adult humans to their precarious and pain-split beginnings in infancy. To do this in any convincing way, the Saviour would himself have to share the same spirit-body, mind-matter, pneumo-psychosomatic existence. He would have to live through all the most painful parts of it, not involuntarily, but willingly, without that splitting-off of the hurt parts from each other in order to make the affliction less unbearable. His willing presence as a Creator who recognized how creation had gone wrong, and wanted to share the predicament and the mess, really would make a difference. . . .

The alongsideness of God himself, as the Author of the whole marvellous yet monstrous creation, would become credible, and a crucial factor in making the reliving of primal pain possible, only if there were some way or ways of his becoming present again, during the turbulent operation of becoming reconciled through all this returning pain . . .

Janov is . . . justified in his statement (p. 196) that 'until they experience deep Primal Pain they cannot know that they have ever deeply felt. The neurotic may think of himself as moral because he has "risen above" anger, but that attitude does not eradicate his anger; it only keeps it buried. . . .' It is 'specious morality. . . . We are only pretending to be moral and it is all sham.' Thus, for neurotics (and this includes all of us who have personality problems, bits of habitual immaturity and 'hang-ups') pain is the avenue to true morality . . . I believe this to be a most important statement and a true one . . . 'Agony is the price of a moral life.'

The CTA and primal integration

To the clergyman offering counselling in the midst of a busy life, or to the counsellor whose main concern is to listen and support, the question of exactly when, in a person's life history, the present distress first took root may seem academic. From his earliest writings, however, FL insisted on its importance. In a postscript to his very first Newsletter, back in the sixties, when all that was at issue was the trauma of birth, he wrote:

The critique that comes . . . from contemporary psycho-dynamics compels those who would devise programmes for mental health *to take account of the human tendency to project both good and bad, the desirable and the undesirable, from out of the heavens and hells of perinatal life, into goals for adult living, failing to recognize their actual origin.* Human adults may think that they are talking about Heaven and Hell, God and the Devil, innocence and guilt, being helpless or all-powerful, saved or damned, when actually they are undergoing an intense replay of one or other of these primal tapes. Naturally, they will use the religions and ideologies that come to hand in order to make sense to themselves and others of these extremely intense perinatal sensations, emotions and relationships.

Primal events are not only superimposed on the commonplace interactions of daily life, but upon theologies and ideologies, upon the central means and ends of human living. In both cases the invasion of primal material causes the most perplexing misperceptions of reality. Adults plunge into courses of action which are determined as to their direction by the direction taken in the primal event. With all the force of Greek tragedy, this strong drive, profoundly misdirected by inner misperceptions of reality, leads to Nemesis or fate . . .

There is a warning of the shift in emphasis that was to come, from training people – and especially clergy – in the conduct of pastoral counselling with individuals, of which 'listening' was the chief ingredient, to group work aimed at enabling individuals to pick up the traces of primal pain.

These past six years of our shared development towards more effective counselling and supervision . . . have been the years during which the Renewal of the Church in the power of the Holy Spirit and in the apostolic gifts for ministry has also been happening among us, and to us . . .

As part of this renewal in the Holy Spirit we are witnessing what is often spoken of as 'Inner Healing', or 'The Healing of the Memories'. As Christians minister to each other, they are able, as a group, to assist those who ask for prayer to open up the trap-doors of repression and the bulk-heads of lifelong dissociations. Hurtful experiences from as far back as birth and babyhood can be thoroughly recovered and relived . . .

Inner healing enables us to bear and thus to integrate the suffering at the source. We can see that a renewed Christianity is undoing the work of repressive religion. Duty-full demands for the suppression of pain and protest, joy and celebration, are being revised in the direction of greater honesty and emotional integrity. This is happening in prayer groups and house groups as well as in the larger gatherings of 'the Renewal'.

In the mid-week conferences of CTA on 'Renewal Prayer Groups and the Healing of Forgotten Pain', these two streams are confluent . . . We now know that these primal tension-generating injuries can be retrieved from the 'tape-library' of birth and babyhood. They can be relived and fully reconnected to consciousness. When this is done, their power and permanence, as dreadful happenings that keep us continually on the run into tension-relieving distractions, is ended.

I am, in all sobriety, affirming that the theoretical and practical means by which groups of Christians are able to do this therapeutic work for each other are already with us . . .[15] It is unthinkable that God the Father should have gone to such lengths, and God the Son to such depths, for us and for our salvation, and [then] left the Holy Spirit without the means to effect that victory in the dark, unevangelized continents of personality which the twentieth century has opened up in the attics and cellars of our experience in birth and babyhood . . .

It may be helpful to quote the distinction FL makes between 'reliving one's birth' and 'being born again':[16]

There has been some suspicion that we have equated the reliving of birth as part of this healing of the memories with the experience of new birth into the family of God by faith in Christ. It is of course not the case . . . There is, however, a very close relationship between the ways in which people encounter difficulty or ease when they come to considering whether they can accept the new birth by faith into Christ or not, since all the fears, doubts and commitment anxieties that beset them at their physical birth tend to crowd round them at the proposal of a second birth. Indeed, to *force* oneself towards the experience of being born again . . . can evoke such disturbances as schizophrenia, if the actual human birth was accompanied by pain of a mind-splitting character . . . Just as Christ healed people physically and left them to decide later what they would do with him by way of faith and discipleship, so, if we can clear the battlefield of the first birth of its living debris, we do at least make it possible for a person to consider the second birth without the degree of panic and confusion, resistance and dread, that accompanied his first birth.

By 1975 there was a wide variety of the short CTA conferences mentioned earlier on offer in Nottingham – in Personal Growth, Marriage Growth, Team Building with Groups at Work, Training Techniques, Journal Keeping for Personal Growth, the Renewal Prayer Group and the Healing of Forgotten Pain, and Personal Growth and Primal Integration in the Small Group – of which the last two were particularly well subscribed. FL reported at length in the *Clinical Theology News* for May, 1977 on the 'wide spread of interests and backgrounds' of those who attended. He also defined his preferred approach to 'Personal Growth and Primal Integration in the Small Group':

Our own particular discipline and training has led us to be able to offer, with well proven knowledge of the indications for it and the results that can be predicted from it, the primal reintegration work that has developed here over the past seven years, with roots into my own practice for more than twenty years. To this we are constantly adding, as the indications for them arise, the whole range of older and newer 'therapies' or growth facilitating methods.

We have therefore decided to join them together, since in practice they refuse to be put asunder . . . It is possible to get 'primal' work, like any other therapeutic or educative method, out of focus. It gives us a new, valuable, and till now almost totally overlooked, entry into the origins of many of our difficulties in being human, loving and real, in such a way as to make us open to change in decisive ways. *It is not and could never be, either the total or final answer.* That waits upon *the ends* towards which we live. To clear up the beginnings can only be a better beginning . . .

'Primal Integration' includes the 'healing' of memories and traumatic experiences by reliving the *sensations* and *emotions* connected with the events, in an awareness of the original *context*. Thorough 'connecting up' of these three elements is what we aim at and, when it happens, the growth is as marked as the relief . . .

We, as the group with the leader, simply facilitate or enable the work to be done. At the end they do not have a feeling of dependence on the group but on their own enhanced powers of bearing, which the group, representing the body of Christ, has made possible.

In *Studies in Restricted Confusion* (p. 3, No. C42) there is a plain statement of the method used:

Primal integration work aims to help the subject to move in sequence through intra-uterine life, from conception to the beginning of bonding with the mother. We evoke the images that represent the anatomical and physiological facts, without making the usual assumption that they leave no traces in cellular memory. It seems that they do.

Some are impressed, even dazzled, by the bliss and brilliance of their entering into the blastocystic phase, before this free, mystical oneness is curbed by implantation. It is at this joining up of the now functioning foetal circulation with that of the mother, with a finger placed on the navel to simulate the cord, that the 'umbilical affect', if it is by no means what the embryo or foetus expects, but in some way bad, is powerfully experienced. It can find expression. In a vivid way, subjects 'recall' how (differently) they dealt with the bad and kept the good.

How they did that would form the basis of their lifelong defensive strategies. Much sensitivity, skill and judgement is needed to make the necessary connections, to be aware of what is happening in the person at work, and to be able to assess his or her power to cope with it in the days that follow. Yet, by the end of his life, FL's model for working with disturbed people had changed from that of the well-trained counsellor and client to that of groups providing mutual care:[17]

... I say mutual not because both are working at recovery and integration at the same time, which would be foolish to attempt, but because the one who today is being cared for tomorrow or the next day will be providing the care. There is no class or category of counsellors, with a separate category of counsellees. That would be alien to the whole spirit and validated experience of the mutual care groups. The work of integration is tough and the confidence to do it with surety is not easily come by. Certainly one of the prime assets of the mutual care communities is that each person regularly explores their competence as an afflicted person being assisted, by the presence of another, to effect the reliving and integration, and also of being on another occasion in the responsible assisting role. There can be no loss of self-esteem here ...

Persuasive as these arguments were, not everyone was happy with the changes that had taken place in the teaching and practice of Clinical Theology, from attempting to understand and come to terms with deep, archaic personal feelings, to the more perilous and time-consuming project of actually 'reliving' and 're-owning' those feelings. There were practical difficulties for those who had come to CT to acquire the skills to make them better parsons, teachers or social workers. The counselling hour sandwiched between other appointments, the house group sharing at greater personal depth, were of a different order from the primalling conferences FL has described. Many of his adherents, particularly those who had not submitted themselves to the experience, felt confused and alienated. Counselling itself acquired quite a different aspect. Were parishioners to relive their primal traumas on the vicarage carpet?

There were also serious misgivings about the results of such work in hands less competent than FL's, however loving, and fears for the reputation of the Association. A gap opened between those chary of his commitment to the work of primal integration and those deeply, often personally, convinced of its worth.

Here, however, he shall have the last word. The following extracts are from an article on 'The neurological basis of primal integration theory':[18]

I share the conviction [of Freud and Janov] that when at last we have a satisfactory theory of the neuroses and psychoses of man, together with his personality disorders, it will be one which can be expressed in terms of neurophysiological processes. A mile of progress in firm neurophysiological understanding is worth ten of metapsychological theory (super-egos, egos, ids and the like) because the former will not need to be displaced, except by further findings that include it . . .

Not that the materialism that is appropriate to neurophysiological research is competent to judge matters outside its field of competence. It is not. However, my conviction is (and this is a faith-statement, firming up with a sureness in which the totality of my being is involved, as I come to the end of forty years in practice, but is never a thing to be claimed as 'demonstrated' or 'proved' in the way the facts of neurophysiology can be established) that the Incarnation of the Son of God and the Redemptive work of Christ is so thorough an entry into our humanity that the root of our alienation from ourselves, from others and from God, will be found in a totally accurate understanding of the Pain, Fear and Dread by which our primal trust and open selfhood was destroyed. The actual events of each person's fall from an original right-relatedness into a state of alienation are now part of a history which is lost to us . . .

. . . it is when a Man arrives on the human scene who reconstitutes before our eyes that open, undefended, and vulnerable Selfhood, and invites us to participate again in that open-hearted trust towards God and others. . . . that our ego defences rise in unmitigated hatred. We kill the Man who represents too faithfully our own long-lost, open-to-trust, open-to-dependency, open-to-the-hazards-of-contingency, original, Primal Self . . .

My conviction is that the true and faithful record of all these primal injustices, iniquities, recoils, dissociations, shut-downs, by which the open self was displaced, hated, and killed off, and, in its place, the symbolic substitutive activities which fill our ego-centred but self-alienated lives, will be found to be clearly inscribed ('etched' was the word Winnicott used) on the circuits and memory banks of babyhood, infancy and childhood . . .

The Counselling Ministry

THE CURE OF SOULS

In 1960, Frank Lake wrote the Foreword to a book called
A Christian Therapy for a Neurotic World, by E. N. Ducker,[1] a
vicar he described as 'occupied almost wholly from morning
till night in the cure of souls, or, to give it its Greek syn-
onym, in psychotherapy'. In it he makes a strong case for
clergymen to take up this kind of ministry:

Any psychiatrist who has worked for some years within the
National Health Service knows, as I do, that the resources of
psychiatry, though considerable, are limited . . . both as to the
number of diseases for which we have effective remedies and as
to the time the psychiatrist can spend with any one patient. In
many mental hospitals this is . . . on the average about five
minutes a patient per week.

He quotes an eminent psychiatrist[2] as saying that to obtain
psychotherapy for an adult under the National Health Service is nearly as difficult as winning the pools, before going
on to say:

Within British psychiatry there has always been a powerful
undercurrent of resistance against psychoanalytical theory and
therapy. Recent extensions of the effectiveness of physical therapy, especially in relieving the symptoms of depression through
electroplexy, and very recently through a new series of drugs,
have given encouragement to this natural scientific desire to be
able to treat the patient at a safe and comfortable emotional
distance, rather than by personal involvement . . .
  In psychotherapy, the essential 'vehicle' in which any 'medicine' is given is the doctor's own personality. This, and the
wisdom gathered in his training, constitute the medical psycho-

therapist's resources. With these he contrives to meet the disorders of the human spirit. Before he can begin to use these
resources he must make a diagnosis.

About three-quarters of all patients referred to psychiatrists
could be labelled 'depressive'. Such patients are filled with gloom
and guilty feelings, often with apprehension. The spirit is at a
low ebb and there is neither power nor joy.

Most of the remainder of neurotic illnesses could be diagnosed
as anxiety states, phobic states, conversion reactions (nothing to
do with religious conversion) or hysteria. In all these there is a
basic fear of separation from the sources of personal Being.
Anxiety is accompanied by a threat of death to the spirit or some
other unmentionable horror. Apprehension rises to panic at the
approach of this inner threat to 'Being' itself. The patient feels
on the edge of an abyss of dereliction and dread, or that he is
falling into nothing, nothing but mental pain and terror.

The obsessional and schizoid personality patterns prove also
to be, in part, defences against this same dread of identification
with non-being. This second group of psychoneuroses, in which
the peace of the human spirit is shattered by perpetual inner
panic, is not one which, as psychiatrists, we can do a great deal
fundamentally to help, much less to cure. Psychoanalysts would
be diffident, and think in terms of long treatment of doubtful
effectiveness in the majority of these cases. Drugs can alleviate
and tranquillize, but tend to cause addiction. Our psychiatric
resources are most inadequate to the healing task for such people.

A third category of emotionally disturbed persons who are
referred to psychiatrists, comprises those who suffer from personality and character disorders of a psychopathic kind. They suffer,
but they make society suffer too. These patients cannot make or
sustain good personal relationships. The normal capacity to love
and be loved has been shattered in the earliest years of life and
distorted patterns of hate and distrust persist. Here too, as
mental hospital psychiatrists, we find our personal resources of
little avail. Only love with firmness, in a suitable family group,
can, in time, heal such people . . .

The fourth category comprises those whose minds have lost
contact with reality. They are of 'unsound mind'. For the most
part these suffer from schizophrenia. They too need not only the
tranquillizing of the disturbed layers of the unconscious mind,
they need loving community and understanding care . . .

Here then, we have the four major categories of mental pain

and disorder, in which what are lost are, successively, joy of spirit, peace of heart, power to love, and the sound mind.

Given the limits to his resources as a psychiatrist, he cries:

... must I not be eager and willing to work with any other professional person who has at his command any resources of the kind my patients need?

For nearly 2,000 years the Church has been drawing attention to the fact that there are resources of love, joy, peace and a sound mind given by God to individuals within her fellowship, through her worship, prayer, and sacraments, and in response to what God is offering to men through the work of the Holy Spirit. The consistent claim of the Church has been that, when people come to an end of their own resources and look away from themselves to what God has been doing in the earthly life, death, and the life beyond death of his Son, they receive, as an inexhaustible resource of personal being and well-being, the Spirit of Jesus within themselves.

It is at the point of greatest 'brokenness' that the gift of right-relatedness to God is often given:

... Christ accepts us in every kind of moral mess or personality disorder, or delinquency that he may find us in. What he never can accept are our delusions of adequacy, our pride in the things we do or think or suppose ourselves to possess. These being broken, as they usually are in those who have fallen so low in their estimate of their social adequacy as to consent to visit a psychiatrist, the way is open to that full acceptance to which Christ, who is God's Good News, invites us.

This moment of brokenness is not only a psychological end-point. It is a precious moment of spiritual truth ... Yet the present state of affairs is such that neither psychiatrists nor clergy are using this crucial moment, with all its potentiality for rebirth and new-being, as it could be used, as it is indeed being used, for instance, by the members of Alcoholics Anonymous ...

In all neurotic sufferers ... this moment of brokenness is potentially, like the death of the phoenix, a moment when new life can arise out of the ashes of the old ... This A.A. talk of brokenness, 'touching bottom', 'admitting that we were power-less' against our problem, and looking to God for strength and new life, with a confidence born of experience of hundreds of thousands that God does work in this way, so that wrecked lives are transformed, all this is too heady and heroic stuff for psychiatrists. Our patients would not thank us for pricking the human bubble. Our task is to blow it up where it sags, or reduce the tension if it strains to bursting. We are in danger of saying 'Peace' when there is no peace. The psychologist is more accustomed to leading the patient towards painful insight, but few specimens of this rare bird ever nest much north of the Thames . . .

But what, he asks, of the clergy and the cure of souls entrusted to them for many generations?

The fact is that popular opinion as to what the parson is for does not usually include the idea that he is a person to go to with a personal problem . . . it would be easier to talk to the doctor. It probably would be! At least he has been taught to listen, and knows that, if he has time, he ought to . . . The clergyman . . . is at present given no such training.

He commends Eric Ducker because, though well versed in psychoanalytic theory, he does not depend on psychoanalytical resources alone for his cure of souls.

. . . He takes the patient down to the spiritual roots of the human predicament, to re-experience, for instance, the dread of death by separation from the source of being, in forsakenness and dereliction. Only at this depth of need does the depth of Christ's redemptive resourcefulness become apparent. Here, where the full agony of mental pain is felt, the agony of the cry of Christ upon the Cross, emerging from the hell of forsakenness, assures the sufferer that though he has gone down into hell, Christ is there in the same hell with him. Moreover, Christ's forgiveness of those whose rage murders him is assurance to all those depressives, whose unconscious aggression against life would slay right and left if it dare, that even his murderers are beloved. By this mighty resource of the Gospel, Christian therapy can give assurance that the divine love outlives and out-manoeuvres all that hate can do . . .

WHAT MAKES FOR GOOD COUNSELLING?

Before Frank Lake's book *Clinical Theology* 'revolutionized' pastoral counselling (to use the words of the *Church Times* review quoted earlier), there appear to have been few pastors equipped to take up the role of Christian therapist in the manner of E. N. Ducker. It is to be hoped, however, that fewer today would approach counselling as FL found them doing in 1967:[3]

Judging by the treatment I receive when I am role-playing the part of a Christian on the edge of depressive breakdown, many priests still tend to take up judgemental attitudes and tell me what I 'ought to have done' or 'must try to do'. I must try not to be depressed. I must try to help someone. I must be more particular about my prayers. I must redouble my efforts not to think angry thoughts or impure thoughts. I must go steadily on without self-pity. I must be more diligent, dispelling tiredness by a little extra hard work. I must make a rule and keep it more diligently.

This may be excellent religious first aid. It is so contrary to psychiatric practice as to account for the desire of many psychiatrists to keep such priests out of their wards. And they should be kept out. Because if the Christian gospel is true, this kind of advice is damnable . . . The common run of 'pastoral advice' deserves Job's derisive comment to his moralistic counsellors, 'Miserable plasterers are ye all.'

Good listening was the foundation of his own teaching. The pamphlet on *Listening*, the first to be issued to seminar members in the early days, began like this:

Why have clergymen been educated and pushed into relative ineffectiveness as personal counsellors, until only the exceptional man is used by his fellow clergy and the laity of the Church in this intimate pastoral task? How has it come about that he has been set aside in favour of the doctor, who is equally untrained in counselling? Have we to make a case for a return to a lost image of the pastor as counsellor? If theological training had not lost its Galilean accent on persons encountered by the roadside or on the roof-tops, in favour of libraries and essays in the schools, it would be unnecessary to argue the case for pastoral listening and dialogue.

To the 1969 edition of the pamphlet FL added a leaflet called *A Training Method for Counselling*,[4] which offers ways of evaluating the quality of listening offered, in role-play, by the trainee counsellor. The texts chosen do away with any idea of the counsellor as the all-knowing authority:

'So the Spirit lifted me up, and took me away, and I went in bitterness, in the heat of my spirit, but the hand of the Lord was strong upon me. Then I came to them of the captivity at Tel-Aviv, . . . and I SAT WHERE THEY SAT, and remained there astonished (dumfounded) among them seven days.' Ezekiel 3:10–15.

'And if you understand the art of making yourself nobody in a conversation you get to know best what resides in the other person.' Kierkegaard

The seminar members given the task of observing and commenting on the counselling role-play are asked to keep the following questions in mind:

1. Does the counsellor make and sustain a caring and accepting relationship?
2. Does the counsellor seem to be 'feeling into' the sufferer's state of mind? Does he give himself wholly to the task of understanding the feelings with 'empathy'? Is he able to put that understanding into acceptable words, so that the sufferer is aware of this?
3. Does the counsellor stay with the sufferer down the painful road of memory, letting the troubled person retain the 'steering-wheel' of the conversation?
4. What obstacles to good counselling did you observe?

With a *pre*liminary warning about making any *pre*sumptions about the person being counselled, FL then lists, and gives examples of, thirteen likely obstacles to good counselling. He enjoyed outrageous puns, and here he has fun with the *pre*fixes, which make his list memorable. The obstacles are these:

1. Premature solutions.
2. Pre-judging the issue.
3. Preventing the expression of strong feeling.

4. Predominating personal need to be the man with the answers.
5. Preference for clearly stated problems.
6. Preconceived idea that one's own experience provides the clue.
7. Prevalent pastoral habit of giving 'practical solutions'.
8. Pressure of religious talk to avoid bad feelings.
9. Pre-existing fear of silence.
10. Predictable attitudes.
11. Predilection for scandal.
12. Pre-arranged system for typing people, for quick disposal.
13. Pre-learnt and highly practised counselling techniques

How many counsellors could absolve themselves of every one of these faults?

Later seminar members learned to discriminate between good and not-so-good counselling responses to the words and feelings of the client, sharpening their awareness of how their own physical and mental attitudes, wording and tone of voice might encourage or inhibit further painful disclosures. But the list of obstacles serves as a useful checklist for spotting failures, not only in counselling but in any human encounter that goes awry.

FL was adamant that counsellors should stay with the flow of the client's disclosures, sitting where he or she sits:

. . . Counselling is more than the dipping of a toe in the surface currents of the personality to register their temperature and direction. It is the becoming aware of the whole oceanic complexity of the personality . . . it means taking note of trapped areas of cold water, below the freezing point of fresh water, such as fill the deep basin of the Norwegian sea, but cannot flow into the Atlantic because of a submarine ridge. For so it is with the worst experiences of cold in infancy (the surgical shock of white asphyxia at birth, or the profound hypothermia induced by the British small bedroom and the icy indifference – as it seems – of sleeping parents), they are colder than the cold from which warmth would be a relief. To warm them up by contact with warmer currents would be as agonizing as the return from frostbite. A submarine ridge called dissociation on the one side and repression on the other keeps them apart from the rest . . . [5]

In 1972 an article in a CT Newsletter indicated the changing emphases in the seminar training,[6] which had hitherto concentrated on the teaching of psychodynamic principles and their application to personal and parochial problems. Aware that the blocks that arose in counselling usually originated in areas of the counsellor unknown to himself, FL was using his tutor training conferences to focus more and more on the problems and resistances of the would-be counsellors themselves. Henceforth the three-hour seminars would place as much emphasis on members' personal growth in self-knowledge, and on the practice of effective counselling, as on the teaching element. He comments:

The aim of growth-groups is to extend the reach of the counsellor's own relationships, both inward and outward, and in his response God-ward, a dimension which interpenetrates both. This is a way of claiming the Lordship of Christ, both in the shadowy continents of mood and memory, and in the social arena, from interpersonal relations, to take account of the 'demonic powers' which dominate so many of our social structures.

. . . Counsellors are perhaps most frequently inadequate when the range of their own capacity to feel does not extend to the comprehension of what the counsellee is feeling. We must be secure enough to feel all our own feelings if we are to offer security for others who require to feel theirs in a relationship with us. That is why growth on the part of the counsellor is of primary importance.

Counsellors cannot help a client to grow (in the power to face painful areas and memories previously blocked off) beyond the point which they themselves have reached. They must possess humility, and a willingness to learn more about the effect they have on others. The same is true for the tutors of seminars. All expressed feelings must be honoured:

It has often been my practice to begin a seminar with a Bible study and prayer. I would take it to be important now to discover from the group how they had reacted to this exercise. In any group of clergymen some will share negative feelings when we talk about God or directly speak to him in this context. Others express anxiety if we do not do this. From the point of view of growth, the important thing is that both of these responses will

121

be honoured. One will not be placed above the other. No one should be manipulated into silence because someone else objects, nor manipulated into making a theological utterance because someone will object if he does not. This is secured when the group values and attempts to stay with the group member while he explores these quite powerful feelings, for or against. If this is done, people value the group experience. They do not leave the group unless they are so disrespectful of others that they insist on dominating. In which case they had better not be encouraged to think of themselves as prospective counsellors.

The 'growth' element in seminars was provided by taking members through 'fantasy journeys' and sharing the images and insights gained; through group tasks like the enacting of stories (e.g. that of the Prodigal Son), with heightened awareness of the feelings involved; and through other 'awareness' exercises and 'games' which evoke deep memories and strong individual reactions.

In the same article FL discusses the recent research findings on the efficacy of counselling and psychotherapy in the USA[7] which have influenced him in making these changes:

It is now possible to set our house in order if we wish to. The attitudes which are possessed by those therapists who do their patients good, beyond the level attainable by the controls [*equivalent groups where no therapy was given*] have been identified by Truax, Carkhuff and others. They have further been refined into six basic dimensions of effective counselling by Carkhuff and his co-workers.[8] There was a demonstrable theoretical convergence in all schools of counselling about these desirable factors in the truly effective therapist. They all agreed that *accurate empathy, unconditional acceptance, respect and warmth, concreteness and genuineness* were the likely factors. What is now certain is that those therapists who do offer to their clients these personal qualities are precisely those who are the improvers, while those who conspicuously lack these qualities are identified as those who are actually damaging their patients or counsellees. To these four dimensions are added, as the counselling relationship develops, *acceptable confrontation* and the *immediacy* which can identify here-and-now manoeuvres.

He insisted that the teaching in seminars should be relevant to the members' needs:

For some years now we have been insisting that the urgent personal concerns of the group members should always be put before the concern of the tutor to teach this or that according to the syllabus for the day. This has been felt to be frustrating by those who were eager to amass facts rather than to experience themselves in counselling situations. The important thing seems to be that, whenever a task has been completed, whether a growth group task or counselling practice, or time given to teaching, or an experience of teaching time being crowded out, that the group leader should then give time to all the members to express what it has meant to them to have experienced this proportion, or, anyone might feel, this *dis*proportion of time spent on the varying tasks. This itself is modelling the kind of leadership which is required for growth groups.

Inevitably some of the more concentrated study of the psychodynamic aspects of personality will be lost, which members may have to supply by their own reading. Yet, he says:

It seems . . . that there are many contemporary conceptualizations in relation to counselling which are often as useful as an understanding of personality reactions and psychodynamics. I refer to Berne's Transactional Analysis, to Encounter Group theory, to Bioenergetics, as taught by Lowen, and to Fritz Perls's Gestalt Therapy.

On the tutors themselves, he says:

The leader must himself be involved and be as open to the group as he expects them to be to each other. He must in no sense be a protected person. I do not say that he can use the group as unrestrictedly as its members. He must himself have a support group to which he can go [*for sorting out any strong feelings or difficulties which arise in him and could interfere with his ability to listen to others*] . . . The apostolic leaders of our faith and the Lord himself shared the effect of pastoral care and counselling on their own personalities very honestly within their own 'support group' . . . We must do that also.

Where tutors have become unstuck, or over-involved with seminar members or with one another, it is generally because they have failed to heed this last important warning.

THE CLINICAL THEOLOGIAN

Not all clergymen were expected to take their parishioners, as E. N. Ducker did, back to their 'spiritual roots'. Their task was well laid out in 1967 in two long, cogent articles on 'The threatened nervous breakdown',[9] from which we can offer only fragments. The first concerns 'threatened breakdown requiring referral' and 'impending reactive depressive breakdowns'. FL is encouraging ministers and pastors to feel that they can play an important part at even these very critical moments:

. . . At his [*the pastoral theologian's*] preliminary interview he must decide whether confusion or dismay as to the ultimate meanings of life are integral to this man's threatened breakdown . . . If people in trouble come to a pastor, it must be because their own intuition has led them to believe that at least part of the problem is in his field of concern. That intuition is important, and so we must consider pastoral first aid, not as a preliminary to sending the man elsewhere, but to dealing with him pastorally in greater depth later . . .

So let us say at once that if a troubled person goes to his minister for help in distress and is met with twenty minutes 'first aid' and nothing more, this will almost certainly be of little or no significance to the solution of his basic problem. If it pretends to be a sufficient pastoral response to a man who has, or feels he has, no one else to turn to, the mere application of 'first aid' constitutes a case of pastoral malpraxis. There are few easier ways of insulting a layman who has been wrestling for months over a life problem, than to have it solved by a cocky minister in a few minutes.

FL used to say, 'The first question I ask myself is, Is it sin or is it sickness? Genuine guilt requiring repentance and change, or over-scrupulous neurotic guilt?' He believed that the pastor could cope with the second as well with the first.

After reviewing situations which may require outside help, such as psychotic breakdowns and depressions so severe as to require medical intervention, which the pastor should learn to recognize, the article considers situations in which the clinical theologian can effectively offer help:

... Even where verbal comprehension is lost [*as in a psychotic episode*] we must not infer that non-verbal, symbolic, personal and sacramental acts cannot reach to the 'heart' in helpful ways.

Now that we have mentioned the main sources of breakdown that demand immediate psychiatric help, and the kind of pastoral first aid that knows how to hold a telephone in one hand and talk to a confused man in gestures with the other, we turn to the great bulk of threatened nervous breakdowns, which are nothing more than crises in the course of personality difficulties and disorders, of neuroses (that is to say, fixated emotional difficulties), of character problems, personal conflicts and inadequacies, fears, scruples, compulsions, irrational fears, bad tempers, bad habits, addictions, 'evil thoughts' of a cruel or envious kind, insoluble marital problems and intolerable stresses at work. [*Do note the 'nothing more than'! Ed.*] These are in us all, more or less, but from time to time the unstable life situation of which they are the cause or the result, or both, becomes even more precarious in its balance and we become aware of this. We feel on edge, at the end of our tether. Can we define what it is that is going on here? . . .

It is a fundamental point of all modern thinking on this subject to recognize that 'nervous breakdown' (like 'psychosomatic illness') is an omnibus term (semantically meaningless – the nerves have not broken down) accommodating all kinds of professionals who want to work on it and give to it, or to the parts of it they are trained to deal with, names, so as to integrate their knowledge systematically. Had the academic theologians not moved out of the serious study of pastoral theology in relation to sick people, theology would now have as significant a stake in 'nervous breakdowns' as psychology or pharmacology . . .

A nervous breakdown is threatened whenever 'bad' aspects of the personality, the negativities which threaten some aspect of his self-affirmation, whatever he regards as dangerous, weak or wicked, over-anxious or over-angry, too meek or too murderous, begin to emerge from hiding to upset the uneasy *status quo*. Some of these could be described as *deprivations*: feelings of emptiness or meaninglessness, worthlessness, nothingness, hollowness and the like, connected directly with anxiety, panic, dread, or fear. Others would theologically be described as *depravities*: destructive rage, hatred, envy, jealousy, greed, and lust. The interaction of complex intra-psychic forces and of external factors leads to a breakdown of the existing defensive pattern . . .

After detailed description, with examples, of how this can happen, he goes on:

The actual onset of breakdown occurs roughly at the moment when these all-or-nothing, built-in responses to long-buried painful experiences are resurrected into consciousness so violently that they break down the retaining wall within the mind, and burst like a torrent of angry waters into consciousness. These can be described in the language of the Psalmist or in the language of the clinician. The symptoms are those of mounting tension, apprehension, edginess, touchiness, irritability, fear of disintegration, or of some unmentionable mental 'crack-up'; and as the thing builds up, there is an uncanny dread, with fears of unreality and loss of the self, or some of its essential qualities.

In parallel with these mental disturbances are the physical symptoms of trembling or shaking, palpitation, cold sweating, tension headaches, tight bands round the head or chest, nervous dyspepsia or indigestion, nausea at the thought of food, 'butter-flies' in the stomach, urgent 'calls of nature', restlessness and the like. If these 'physical' symptoms due to autonomic disturbances are at all severe, the doctor can always give useful first aid by way of tranquillizer or sedative to take the edge off these most distressing feelings. *And a skilled pastoral approach which deals with some of the important contemporary sources of anxiety, and may explain simply how the symptoms are due to the reawakening of long-buried anxieties, will have the same pacifying effect.*

FL describes the breaking through of mounting rage, lust, anxiety, distrust and apathy – a weakness of the will to be good – in a man about to suffer a depressive breakdown, and his attempts to disguise these feelings:

Now when this man is himself a pastor, what treatment or advice constitutes good pastoral first aid? Shutting his bad self indoors, the depressed pastor is now, in full view of his parish, pacing back and forth with an earnest look upon his face, on the balcony of his life. Perhaps he is as yet unaware of the energy he is using up every day in resisting the impulse to leap over it to his death . . . He is on the edge of a breakdown, but he cannot admit it . . . He cannot slow up the pace of his good works, because they, and they alone, are shoring up the retaining wall . . . So the first aid he wants, possibly the only first aid he will accept, is such as will help him to maintain his religious front, and for this he will be grateful.

But must we not admit that if all that follows first aid by way of pastoral care is in this same dimension, it is a pyrrhic victory, gained at the expense of a potentially deeper Christian grounding in painful truth and brokenness?

Perhaps what has gone before in this Reader will make it clear what kind of longer-term counselling is needed, since there is only space here for a few paragraphs:

It is impossible to speak of God's peace in counselling a man on the edge of depressive breakdown, or to lead him to that peace, without somehow alluding to the theology epitomized in that devastating text of Paul in Galatians 5:4 [*If you try to be justified by the Law you automatically cut yourself off from the power of Christ, you put yourself outside the range of his grace.*] Without question, this brother is trying to get rightly related to God, that is, to his true source of being, by doing what the law, even though it be God's law, commands. To do this, according to Paul, is simply to 'cut yourself off' from Christ . . .

The pastoral theological therapy for the over-driven depressive man works on the very same dynamic principles as the psychiatric therapy, which consists in rest and all that makes for rest, and then a gradual recreation in all systems. To rest, in despair of oneself, in the loving Being of God, on the invitation of Christ, is possible, for the Holy Spirit makes it so. I think back on many occasions when, within the course of two, or two and a half, hours, a priest or minister, threatened with depressive breakdown, has told me his whole tale and has moved, in the last half hour or so, through into this gracious peace. If we define first aid as that which must be done in under half an hour, I would find myself totally at a loss. But if I am allowed two and a half hours, and perhaps an hour or two on three subsequent occasions, though they may not be necessary, then first aid, so conceived, can conclude the whole operation of clinical pastoral care . . .

His second article is addressed to the care of the anxious person. Though he deals with the terrors both of separation anxiety and of commitment anxiety, the following selection deals mainly with the first:

There are people whose threatened nervous breakdown has no relation to depressive dynamics at all. They are not burdened by the law, duties or a ponderous conscience. The 'badness' which threatens them is not expressed as moral badness but as the 'badness' of loneliness or separation anxiety, of emptiness and meaninglessness. They respond with heightened sensitivity to external life situations which deprive them of good company, or durable friendships and exciting times, or warm and comforting emotions. These needs determine what they look for from the churches they attend. Though appearing to be 'terribly keen on' a multiplicity of social meetings, they are, if the inner truth were declared, in flight from intolerably painful experience of loneliness, right up to the panic of infantile dereliction and dread. Or they are in flight from fixated experiences of weakness, emptiness, or exhaustion, of fearful and persecutory intensity.

In these rather extraverted people, the 'threatened nervous breakdown' is an expression of the weakening of the retaining wall of repression which holds back the deluge of the primal terrors of the abyss, or the aridity of the wilderness. Their natural response to this weakening of the dam is to intensify the activities which have always been in reaction against the specific forms of 'badness' or 'negativity' to which they are prone. They attend more meetings than ever, injecting more apparent enthusiasm into them. They 'can't stand' those who cannot work up an equivalent or superior 'keenness'. This 'keenness' tends to express itself also in the sharp cutting edge of their criticisms of others. The fact is that their peace and joy have been, almost from the beginning of life, negated by fearful inner loss of being or well-being, as persons in relation to others . . .

He describes this in greater depth and then says:

What, then, is true pastoral care for people like this, in whom, in spite of their exacerbated zeal to potentiate and elevate religious sensation, a breakdown of the whole process has become imminent? To palliate would be, perhaps, to arrange for a revival mission, or move to a keener church with more of what it takes to keep loneliness and emptiness at bay. It would be quite mistaken to despise this kind of move . . .

If the symptoms of distress are at all severe, you may need to refer the parishioner as a patient to his doctor . . . But it may well be that as a result of the pastor's patient and attentive listening to the sufferer's tale of trouble, these physical and emotional symptoms of distress decline considerably within the interview. This often happens when a good rapport is established. Listening of the right sort is the basis of first aid in clinical pastoral care . . .

In threatened breakdown we discern an often sharp division between the patients who clamour for pills to rid them of the distress, and those who are deeply relieved . . . when . . . you settle down to listen to them without an eye on the clock. The first group come to clergy for healing magic. Their god is a *deus ex machina* whose job is to deliver them from this or that painful symptom. There have been priests and ministers who could dance to this tune, the intense, ecstatic sort who can pressure a devoted follower into the denial of any symptom. They need each other. But this tends to psychological collusion of neurotic needs, the 'gruesome twosome', not clinical pastoral care . . . If sacramental acts such as the Laying on of Hands is offered to such people, their sole intest is 'Will it work?' . . . This does not invalidate such acts, but it can drag their essentially personal meaning into the gutter . . .

But those who have some 'psychological space', some spiritual depth, perception, insight, realism, introspective honesty, reflectiveness, and capacity for dialogue . . . may move very fast indeed to the point of the paradox . . .

As soon as the Christian realizes that Christ's next appointment with him is not in the world of finitude, touch, or sight, but in the depths from which flight is no longer necessary, precisely that which threatened him throughout his life becomes that which invites him as a pilgrim to proceed on his journey, in Christ, to meet Christ, in the total 'darkness' of the 'absence' of God, for this is an authentic mode of the vision of God which is the end of our human journey . . .

A language that comprehends painful experience

Much has been said about listening to, and not preaching at, people who come for pastoral help. So what kind of language is appropriate to their needs? The following passage from an early Newsletter offers one answer:[10]

Those who are undergoing mental pain speak in a language which comes instinctively, which is common to all sufferers. They speak of their terror of waves and storms, of the quicksands' clutch, of feet stuck in mud, of being turned to stone, of the fires through which they must pass to safety, of occasional shafts of ineffable light, soon lost again in the darkness but never forgotten, of paroxysms and storms of terror, giving place to calm and peace of mind, and perhaps, in the end, of a kind of joy in bearing each day's, each moment's, inevitable suffering without complaint or bitterness. They may speak of a new intimacy with. God, experienced as personal love and infinite concern, and blush lest we should think of them as qualifying for the diagnosis of mania, or presumptuous sainthood. The fluency with which some who are in irremediable affliction have learned to use the ultimate, unscientific language of creative suffering, has taught some doctors to welcome it, both for other patients and for themselves.

There are many whose minds have been invaded by the intolerable pains and helpless passivities of infancy, or by the fragmentation and 'distortion' of schizophrenic thinking. They cannot repel the invasion, and no medical skill can assure them that they will ever recover without possibility of relapse. Of course, it is the duty of those who work with scientific language to work on in their own attempts to eradicate the evil itself . . .

There is no virtue, however, in refusing to be bi-lingual. While the language of science speaks in terms of isolation of evil and its eradication, and the Bible at times speaks in a similar sense, it also . . . is full of the same language which patients use. In fact, the Bible contains a language which only comes into its own when it is applied to those who suffer from the experiences we associate with breakdowns of one sort or another. It, too, speaks of waves and sinking, fire and purgation, dark nights in the soul, the wilderness of facelessness and terror and lust, anxieties of commitment and loneliness, of principalities and powers, of demonic forces, of darkness and celestial powers of light.

So effective, however, have been the cultural forces which have seized the right to interpret the experiences of breakdown exclusively in scientific terms, that those who suffer have been separated from the only language which would make sense of their suffering in the long run. Clergymen still refer to this symbolic language and to its message of a creative passage through suffering and evil, as they read it in the Psalms, in the words of Christ and elsewhere. But neither they nor their congregations seem to have connected the language and its message with the regularly occurring phenomena of neurotic and psychotic disturbance. When these experiences come upon a member of the congregation, he does not, with quiet eagerness, say to himself, 'Here, at last, are the experiences to which the language I have listened to every Sunday has referred, and to which I was, until now, a stranger.' Precisely at this moment he regards his disturbing experiences as something which must at all costs be hidden from his fellow worshippers and from his pastor. Head bowed with shame, he takes himself off to the doctor and on to the psychiatrist . . .

> To change the climate of churches, or church groups, which make him feel he needs to do this, and to reconquer, for the clergyman, the ground lost to the medical doctor: this is what Clinical Theology is all about.

Prayer

> Counsellors daunted by the magnitude of their task may find comfort and inspiration in this excerpt from one of FL's first Newsletters to the membership of CTA:

The goal of prayer is the 'vision' of the face of God in Christ. Were we dependent on our introversial moods, the only honest report some of us could give is that our 'god' is faceless, and has therefore never helped us to be a person, or become a proper or a happy one. The glory of God's face which breaks into view in the face of Our Lord Jesus Christ is that he warmly accepts us *with* and *in* all our negativities. To hold before our eyes his countenance towards us, as shown so clearly in his life and passion and resurrection is, at one and the same moment, perfect activity and perfect rest. In this prayer of simplicity, though it moves on from words and pictures to wordlessness and the loss of all images, lies the only ultimate healing of that broken humanity which lies behind our 'nervous breakdowns'. Some have 'breakdown' thrust upon them. The Christian's wisdom is to avert or heal 'breakdown' by 'brokenness' before the compassionate countenance of God.

To this paradox we add another. Other people will be healed in our presence only in so far as our attitudes, and our facial expression of them, bear the marks of Christ's own, an eager readiness to unite himself and identify himself with the truth about us, which is invariably, if all the inner truth be told, shameful. The growing points of any personality are always those which our instinct is to hide from critical gaze. Forgiveness waits upon a sense of sin, the fullness of the Spirit's indwelling waits for an admission of emptiness. God's timeless being is assimilated only in so far as death in non-being is realized. So we, with his mind in us, welcome any tentative expression of 'negativity' in others, and encourage its full expression. Only through this paradox can their truth or healing come . . .

And also this, from his first Report from the Research Department in 1978:

Whatever has to do with the deepest meanings and values of life, such as our ultimate concerns and eternal assurance, exerts a profound effect on the grounds of the outcome of pastoral care and counselling. We can 'taste and see' how gracious the Lord is, but what we taste and what we see with the eyes of faith and vision cannot be proved statistically to be more advantageous than following the world's invitation to eat, drink and be merry. There is a qualitative difference between the relief from anxiety given by an efficient tranquillizer and that which comes from the paradoxical peace of God. His peace embraces more anxiety than it suppresses. The difference counts, but it cannot be counted. We can 'research' the roots and the fruit of these different standpoints, but to attempt to computerize the findings would be futile. The Judge is patient and the judgement not yet obvious. God's truth disturbs us before we recognize it as deliverance.

8

Sexuality and Spirituality

SEXUAL IDENTITY

Clinical Theology lays more emphasis on the need for good and loving relationships than on the need for sexual fulfilment, though the repressive barriers we erect can, of course, cause equal devastation in both areas. Two lectures delivered in the late sixties to Cambridge students specifically addressed the matter of sexuality. They were called 'The Sexual Aspects of Personality'[1] and 'Personality, Sexuality and Morals'.[2] These were the 'swinging' sixties, the spectre of AIDS had not reared its ugly head, and young people were plunging into sexual relationships almost without asking themselves if this was what they really wanted. Frank Lake did not pretend to any special expertise. In the Chapel of St John's College, he began:

Most of us are genuinely in the dark when we look to see what is right and wrong about our sexuality. Sex is a religious issue, a moral issue, and a psychological issue. Each of these has its experts but their record is not such that we can regard any of them as consistently able to illuminate the sexual scene.

There is one development, however, in all three fields, which I think we may well hope is here to stay, namely the widespread recognition that rigid repression of the sexual urge is a sick answer, morally bad, religiously pharasaical, and psychodynamically a source of destructive conflict inside the person and between persons. Jesus went to great lengths to uncover the hidden corruption that underlies so much that passes as religious and moral virtue. He didn't come, he said, to call the virtuous into the Kingdom of God, but the sinners, the sexually preposterous, and the secular traitors in the pay of the Romans. He was crucified, in part, because these were truths revealed before their

133

time. Mary Magdalene came to Jesus out of the night of moral and religious condemnation laid down by the Establishment.

We are perhaps only a little less in the dark, even though our sexual experimentation can now be allowed in many circles as common to parents and children, to authorities in state and university as well as to students. The discovery of the unconscious has underscored everything that Jesus is recorded as saying. The old ethic recognized the sexual as one of the great motivational forces of human behaviour, potentiated at times by the demonic powers issuing from the collective unconscious. But, having said, 'Know thyself' as a sexual being, the old ethic quickly added, 'And now, hide thyself'.

The absolutely successful form of hiding the sexual self from the conscious self is repression. The backlash of repression has been severe, in the prudery that has ruined thousands of marriages, and complacently condemned thousands of so-called 'fallen women', in the denial of the body that has impoverished whole cultures and reduced the level of warmth and emotional outgoing we could permit in our families and communities to a cerebralized or formalized trickle.

The lid is off now. The old ethical standpoint is untenable . . . The human race is now in danger on the other side, of being disintegrated by the 'moral insanity' that has taken possession of it. This is itself a symptom of a transitional period lacking any ethic. The answer is not to put the old ethical lid on again. We are in the dark, a genuine and mostly honest darkness, and whoever we come to for the answers, we come, like Nicodemus, by night . . . [3]

In his address in Great Saint Mary's Church, he said:

My task is, I take it, to comment usefully on the related fields of personality development and sexuality. This is a subject . . . on which it is very difficult to know whether you are being honest or not. In these discussions our emotions tend to be more in evidence than our intelligence, and when our irrefutable logic goes to work most furiously, it is often to cover up unacceptable emotions. We are apt to be least honest when we are attempting to put a case so persuasively as to win a verdict in favour of our official standards. This I could not do, because there is so much that I am not sure about . . . In these matters there is little to be gained . . . by the reiteration of what, in our minds as moralists, ought to be. We can make a more useful comment by keeping closely to what is . . .

There is no area of knowledge in which communication is inherently so difficult. We live in different universes because temperament, personality, and sexual choice vary so widely. I cannot see you, who are in front of me now, with the eyes of a woman, or understand you with the mind of a woman and its particular universe. Even if you who are women are rebelling against the woman's universe in favour of a masculine one, it still isn't my universe. I do not possess the advantage of some of my homosexual friends, of lifelong practice in looking at human beings as if I were the woman I wanted to be . . .

If I were to suggest, as Freud tended to do, that the two fields of personality and sexuality are almost synonymous and co-extensive, many of you would readily agree. And I am not referring only to those of you whose friends would consider your personality too sexy for safety. Those of you whose personalities have been richly and harmoniously developed, as the excellent natural product of strong and supportive mothering and fathering in a sound family with brothers and sisters would, I think, agree on reflection that personality and sexuality begin together and develop together almost from birth. Even to the mother, her baby is not just a baby, it is clearly . . . a baby boy or a baby girl . . . All she does for it bears this difference in mind.

He describes how good parenting helps to give the child a clear sexual identity in adulthood:

There are, so to speak, doors in the unconscious, behind which stand the eternal forms of the man and the woman, the mother and the father, the wife, the husband, the wise old man, and the wise old woman. Each of these doors has a lock which is, say, father-shaped or mother-shaped. They can be opened only by an actual human mother and an actual father. The entrance of the baby into the experience of being properly mothered and genuinely fathered turns these potentialities into actualities . . .

Our whole personality is compounded of these two elements. The family life which is the core of all our basic experience of ourselves is inescapably compounded of male and female. There is a sort of appropriateness in the unusual phrase in Genesis that, 'God created man in his own image, in the image of God he created him, male and female created he them.' All human life begins where the identity of every baby begins, or should begin, as a derivative of female and male elements, of mothering and fathering. In this sense personality and sex are coterminous.

THE ORIGINS OF PERSONALITY AND SEXUALITY

To explain how sexuality develops, FL takes his audience back to the Womb of the Spirit.:

The human baby has an infinite longing for human companionship. It does not only feed on the breast, it feeds on the face of the mother. We come to life in the light of a loving countenance. This is where we gain identity, being, and well-being as persons . . . But all hope and expectation, when too painfully frustrated, leads to separation panic, and this in the end turns into its opposite, a terror that one is *not* separated from so painful a predicament as waiting for a Godot who never comes.

Here we have a 'pre-sexual', that is, in the Freudian sense, a 'pre-genital phase' problem, in the first year of life, which profoundly affects both personality and sexuality . . .

He describes the infant's identification with its mother:

. . . To exist in the certainty of the reappearance of the mother's face and arms and breast is to be identified with personal being. If the face is loving, the arms gentle, and the breast ample, this is to be identified with well-being . . .

As you can realize, if the mother, because of her own personality difficulties, has none of these attributes and, by contrast, the baby's father is substituting for her in the mothering role, attentive, patient, available, welcoming, encouraging, then a sexual differentiation has been laid down in the first year. Even if the father is only slightly less intolerable than the dreadful mother, a pattern of homosexual preference may be laid down in the baby boy.

It is precisely in late adolescence, when the support of the family and the tutelage of the school fall away, that the choice of a role in life demands a re-examination of identity. A new beginning has to be made. A new relationship has to be set up which is to be the basis of a new family. Everything is beginning again and all the experiences of the first year reverberate. If the first year has been supportive and strong, and not contradicted too fundamentally by subsequent years, we expect a smooth passage through these narrows. If, at this age, we have no

136

identity, if nothing else constitutes our humanity than that which our human parents have given us, we may well be determined, inflexibly, for or against personal involvement, for or against marriage.

Assuming that his Cambridge audience will be largely made up of people whose personality defences were of the hystero-schizoid type, FL speaks of the personality and sexuality 'split into two opposing camps by dread', 'in the grip of two contrary anxieties whose remedies are incompatible'.

The young man, urged on from within by a dreadful need to overcome his tensions by sexual oneness with a girl, wants to assuage his own separation anxiety in sexual intercourse. But his commitment anxiety puts the wind up him at the very thought of marriage. The girl, more hysterical than autistic, dreads, it is true, commitment to pregnancy and an unwanted baby, she may even have some qualms of conscience, but she dreads even more his threat to drop her if she refuses him. He has become her very being, and without him she feels herself slipping down into the abyss again. This threat prevails, her objections are overpowered and she consents.

He cites a clergyman who 'made five attempts to commit himself to marriage, with five successive girls in five successive parishes' and only at the sixth attempt, and 'by dint of some therapy', made it finally to the altar:

No personality problem I know of frustrates the onward development of a truly integrated personal and sexual life so inexorably as this splitting by dread. It causes profound unhappiness, and most of our makeshift solutions, including the Freudian psychoanalytic ones, evade the issue and perpetuate the splitting. It is perhaps the commonest source today of unresolved marital conflict . . .

He then takes up the matter of primal injuries:

I must ask you to go back with me even one stage further and realize that personality and sexuality are profoundly influenced by what goes on even in the birth passages in the middle stage of labour. [*In later years he would almost certainly have traced this primal dread further back into the womb.*] What is painful to the mother may be so painful as to be lethal to the baby's spirit even though it survives . . .

. . . Since the mother is secretly the focus of . . . dread, the infant's mounting confidence, which the mother does most to achieve . . . does not alter the basic verdict against her . . . Three-quarters of my homosexual patients who have undergone . . . analysis [*under LSD–25*] have discovered the psychodynamic origins, both of their profound distrust of women and their hysterical clinging to men, in birth trauma and subsequent events in the first year of life. Some babies are so damaged and autistic at birth that they never trust anyone thereafter. Their treatment is exceedingly difficult and prolonged. Of course there are genetic and constitutional factors involved, but it is the psychodynamic ones which determine the object-choice and the splitting of personality.

Since these things are so, it is untrue and unfair to state, as the Wolfenden Committee did, that it is no more difficult to control or break off homosexual relationships than to control or break off those of normal heterosexual love. Unless, of course, the Committee were of the opinion that all heterosexual relationships are between persons similarly split by dread and driven by it to irresistible passion and irresistible aversion to solitude. No; the unsplit, unstressed person is not driven as these are, by dread, to trembling sexual impatience and importunity.

The therapeutic predicament. Well, what is the answer to all this? The present trend is towards an increase (judged by all the indices we have available) of personalities so stressed by this and that in infancy as to be conditioned by dread and its compulsions. Society is modifying its standards to accommodate them, which seems at first to be only reasonable since they did not ask to be split. So, premarital sex without commitment occurs oftener and earlier, egged on by aphrodisiac inoculations on almost every channel of communication and advertisement. This, in spite of the pill, etc., is giving another dreadful hell of an unwanted beginning to life to thousands of babies every year . . .

Sociologically, this easy bending and breaking of obligations and relationships whenever the chill wind of dread blows is no doubt regrettable. Until it is our own dread's turn to make us break the rules, we are either for the rules, or, for an equally dread-determined reason, in favour of moral anarchy. But to urge moralistic standards against fornication and adultery, desertion and infidelity, lovelessness and callous neglect in families, is a waste of time when a greater dread than the sanctions of the law can command drives you to break the law.

Is there no re-uniting of our divided selves, no relief for the splitting, no creative entry into dread? Is this the destiny of man, to grow backwards into his roots, to take the pantheistic road which leads back to the sub-personal nirvana of the womb, to gain security from the uncanny in nature mysticism? Or, avoiding the depths altogether, to strengthen his defences in a variety of extravert or introvert positions either side of the abyss? Or, like so many of us in the helping professions, to attempt to straddle the abyss, giving ourselves and withdrawing ourselves from people at one and the same time, tidily, decorously, but inexorably limited in our commitment? These are all evasions.

What is stronger than dread? In the long term of Judaeo-Christian experience, it is 'the fear of the Lord' which is the beginning of wisdom, the ground of right conduct, and the backbone of interpersonal dealings. It is the fear of the Lord which sets all other fears aside and keeps us on an obedient course when the force of temptation on either side runs high . . . It is an adoring reverential trust of him and his nature as it is revealed . . . And in response to his revelation of himself to us, we are given that power of being which can pursue an undeviating course of obedience right through the dark valleys of dread, and under the overwhelming waters of confusion and mental pain, with a sustained zest because of the joy which is set before us. This is the joy of being whole again in him, made one, reconciled to ourselves and to others, in single-heartedness, or to give it its technical term, 'made holy'.

. . . That is what salvation is about. By his Spirit, interpenetrating ours, a new power of endurance comes into force, so that the trial is never more than, in him, we can bear.

SEXUALITY AND RESPONSIBILITY

The later lecture, too, asks how much of the past is present when young people experience themselves as falling in love:

. . . among the young men and women who come up to this university, there are many for whom parental love . . . has been so deficient in its operation that they are here and now, in the university, seeking an identity through experience of these basic roles. To say that this agenda should have been completed before they left home is to confuse the ideal, rare enough nowadays, with the actual. Your rather high suicide rate is an indication that some are so disappointed in their search for people to whom to relate for a satisfactory identity, that to wait on, hanging about for a Godot who never comes, has become unbearable.

So when you, a young man, meet a girl your own age, and she responds to your kindliness with interest and affection, what do you think it is that she wants? . . . It may be that she wants a lover, but I beg of you to remember that it may be a father, or a brother, or even, since we can look across the sexes for help if we need it urgently enough, for the basic 'mothering' that makes her a human being at all. Are you prepared to be the responsible one who takes the trouble to ascertain what it is that at present she feels most in need of? Are you capable then of that restraint on the one hand, and generosity on the other, that lets the friendship develop in such a way that you become the guardian of her freedom to say 'no' to that for which she is not yet ready? It may cost you a lot, but I think this is what love is, to be the guardian of the other's integrity . . .

All this means that we need to recognize the multiplicity of the personal agendas that are being, and have to be, worked through by young people with young people, only some of which, the minority, can appropriately move to a conclusion in sexual intercourse. Be aware of these unfinished tasks of family loving in each other, and respect them, or great confusion and breakdown may ensue.

Above all, we need to learn a skill not taught in schools . . . of becoming aware of the nature of our relational needs, and learning to put them into words, to help each other make the distinctions that love needs to make. There is much that militates against this self-disclosure and openness . . .

Self-disclosure has become so important that its practice has become a moral issue. We have a responsibility to others and to ourselves to define, and if necessary re-define, what it is we are seeking in a relationship. This isn't easy for us to do. The essence of neurotic illness could be expressed as being too afraid or too guilty to put words to, or give expression to, our own real feelings and needs, and therefore what we want out of this or that relationship. We are conditioned to self-concealment, but nowadays, when literature, drama, the mass media, and our common speech are owning up much more frankly to the emotions that in more rigidly religious ages had to be disavowed, we are helped in this basic requirement of mental health and moral integrity. Self-disclosure – even to the point of disclosing that there is only an almost non-verbalizable despair and nothingness at the heart of 20th-century man – has won for Samuel Beckett a Nobel Prize for Literature . . .

. . . the free spirit grows with self-disclosure to others and acceptance by them of all that has to be known. As the spirit grows by honest intimacy, the fruits of the spirit – love, joy, peace, patience, temperance, and endurance – make for that kind of relationship that is so satisfyingly rich already, that without any great sense of frustration the young man and woman can, if they so choose, or feel so called, delay the sexual culmination of their love until their exchange of vows has sealed their love with a life-long intention to fidelity.

Here, as in the earlier address, he proposed Christ as the only reliable healer for the person split by dread:

Those for whom a hectic intercourse is an antidote to the tension of dread and disintegration are not to be dissuaded from it by any authority, if the burden of their objections to carnality are on moral grounds alone. The weaponry of dread has always a bigger calibre than moral cannonry. If, however, the dissuader is Jesus Christ himself, his offered dynamic is no longer a stream of thin-blooded objections in the hardened oughteries of authority, it is a dynamic that can make us what he is, a bloody victor whose body submitted willingly to the commitment agony of Gethsemane and the separation-dereliction of Golgotha, and all that lay between of demonic attack; whose broken body now exists for ever in the memory of the Church, reaching down into the crevices of our existence, and is for ever alive and with us. In him, we can become responsible in the very place from which all compulsive sexual irresponsibility and impetuosity arises . . . Your goal is now no longer to get out of it all by one transcendental experience or another, by sexual orgasm and ecstasy, or a good trip back into the womb of mystical absorption on the wings of LSD. Your goal is to respond to a good-neighbourly relationship, since God in Christ has become our neighbour when we visit the dark recesses of dread and the demonic. Your goal is to be related to Christ and to live in Christ wherever he happens to be leading you. Since he fills all heavens and all hells, you need not fear disclosing to him, or to his, where you actually are. Painful self-disclosure becomes possible at the Cross, which reconciles the sufferer and forgives the sinner . . .

He concludes by saying (though his words here are much abridged):

I cannot regard it as reasonable or feasible to demand life-long marital fidelity, or premarital restraint somewhere before the full act of intercourse, on moral, religious or psychological grounds. The personality drives against such demands overwhelm all the armaments that the moralists and the religious can muster. The last word, therefore, is not with religion in general. Religion is the psychoanalyst's bugbear and he, of all people, has reason to be grateful to Christ who, as Paul says, kills the law and puts an end to the law's requirements on us . . . [4]

. . . We come, like Nicodemus, to Jesus in the night of our true condition. We need more than the bridling of our appetites, we need the new birth. And this, in spite of all religion and morality, is his gift. It is, I think, only within the framework of this new being and our ethical response to his life within us that Christians, puzzled as all men are about their sexual loving, yet discern a presence and a voice, a direction and a power, unimpeded by the darkness of the night.

SAME-SEX LOVING

FL saw the tendency to form attachments with persons of one's own, rather than the opposite, sex as having its roots mainly in primal dread. He considered it, therefore, susceptible to change if desired, though not easily and only by dint of prolonged therapy. However, if the capacity for human loving is not impaired, a homosexual orientation is in itself less damaging to the personality than extreme schizoid detachment, though its social concomitants may be more troubling.

The subject of homosexuality, as FL understood it, is dealt with in *Clinical Theology* and in *Tight Corners in Pastoral Counselling*. In addition, an article called 'The homosexual man',[5] clearly lays out the issues with which the pastoral counsellor is confronted and the limitations to the help that can be offered. A note at the end points out that since 'only one in a thousand among homosexuals requiring help can obtain full therapeutic treatment from a psychiatrist . . . the help a minister or pastoral counsellor must give will not be "first aid" but rather the total help available to the man in need.'

142

The stereotyping that bedevils counselling. The time to start giving first aid to a homosexual person is not at some future date when we may be consulted by a man suffering in one of the many crises associated with the homosexual condition. The ability to help then depends largely on the extent to which we have been able already to shake ourselves free of the many misconceptions and prejudices which tend to have imposed themselves upon us. These come from within our own personalities and from many external pressures of public opinion, which have stereotyped all homosexual men in terms of the most delinquent members of the fraternity. This devaluation of a whole class of men by imposition of a stereotype is not only false to the findings of psychiatry and sociology, as disciplines attempting to keep contact with facts, it is a myth we unconsciously foster to keep our own homosexual elements rigorously dissociated from our self-awareness, as 'not me at any price'. But the price of our rather suspect denial and ruthless projection is the creation of a kind of open prison in the midst of an apparently free society, in which all those who can be identified with the accusation (not now, we note, 'diagnosis') of 'homosexual', have been, without possibility of appeal, condemned and put away behind the bars of social ostracism, imprisoned there for life . . .

Non-recognition of the problem. Four out of five of those men whose erotic desire is towards their own sex, and averted from women, are not recognizable by others as having this homosexual deviation . . . So, unless the majority disclose their particular secret propensity to the counsellor, it cannot be certainly known by observation of general behaviour. From this we conclude that the pastor will counsel many, if not most, of his homosexual parishioners without realizing that homosexuality is part of their problem . . .

Clarifying some practical issues in Christian counselling. It is because his congregation, as well as his parents and long-forgotten teachers, are looking over his shoulder, monitoring his mind, that many a minister feels compelled to condemn the acts of homosexual love with a horror which the New Testament writers express equally, or more so, towards pride, blasphemy, rejection of little children . . . lovelessness, and contempt of others, all of which flourish in the congregation without comment. The minister who welcomes homosexual persons in the name of Christ, unconditionally, must often reflect that a like acceptance could not be expected from his congregation. If they knew what he was doing, they would condemn him . . . But the homosexual man has a right to know, in these uncharted seas, to what port our own system of values would steer him, should he invite us on board as co-pilot . . .

A homosexual orientation is so common at one stage or another of a boy's growth, from infancy to the end of adolescence, as to be regarded by many as a normal stage of development. Having attained heterosexual maturity as an adult, we hope that a happy marriage will seal a man's love of the woman, one woman, as the permanent way of his sexuality. But every 'nervous breakdown', or 'insurmountable emotional crisis' in life tends to turn a baffled man back upon his tracks to look over the possibility that earlier ways of solving the problems of living and loving may again be valid. This is the mechanism of *regression* and, as such, it implies the return to the emotional perspectives of years gone by . . .

I have been called in to give a medical opinion in a number of court cases of clergymen involved in homosexual acts or of 'loitering with intent' round public lavatories. In every case these men had for many years attempted to face up to life squarely on as adequate a level of emotional adjustment as they could manage, but the scandalous loneliness of the single clergyman, in his totally uncared for cure of souls, had literally 'got them down'. One man was so irremediably isolated . . . that he pictured prison as a heaven of closeness and friendliness, with men equally despised as he was, and equally lovable . . .

In that case, the specific 'problem' was loneliness and depression rather than homosexuality. FL goes on to say how he would expect to behave to a homosexual client. What follow are only the headings, on which he enlarges at some length:

I would aim to enhance such heterosexual leanings as he already has, and diminish the time and energy spent in homosexual fantasy and its acting out in homosexual genital, anal or masturbatory intercourse.

Accepting the fact that in many cases the homosexual choice cannot be dislodged, then, far from devaluing it, I [would] regard its lovingness as a powerfully good asset in the personality.

Whether I put this into words or not, I would feel that the aims of 'therapy' would be furthered by his continued deep friendships with both men and women on all the levels of loving that are compatible with his own and his society's acknowledged patterns of loving.

I would set about correcting the false image of the 'god' of the religious who regards sexuality of both sorts as so tainted with evil as to be itself sinful.

What FL says further under this last heading, about relieving neurotic guilt feelings, demands inclusion:

The equation of sex=sin is terrible enough in its ruinous effects on those who can marry, but it is more terrible in the burden of guilt it brings upon the mind and heart of the homosexual man. The psychodynamic origins of homosexuality in both its components, of schizoid withdrawal from sexuality with women and hysterical clinging toward men, are so early in their onset . . . that all the 'badness' of the mother-baby relationship is interpreted by the baby as 'my own, unaccountable . . . inalienable badness'. No suffering or evil in babyhood is attributed to the mother alone. The innocent baby interprets the 'badness' as personal badness=guilt. This is not a moral guilt that could be 'atoned for' by repentance or reparation. It sticks as a feeling in spite of all 'forgiveness'. Much of the counsellor's effort can usefully go into interpreting and removing these neurotic guilt feelings, since homosexuality as a particular sexual orientation is never chosen by anyone, it is chosen for them by particular combinations of factors, genetic and constitutional (relatively unimportant), familial, parental and social (very important) over which there could be no control or choice.

His last two points are these:

This caring of ours need not cease even if the priest, minister, or doctor is asked to share the burden of knowing about illicit liaisons, past or present . . . our wrath works no righteousness. To give him the reasons why you believe his course of action to be wrong . . . is in my view quite necessary . . . [But] we do not add to his self-contempt by ours. Christ's care in us continues along with his judgement.

I trust that the net effect of my counselling will be to enable changes to take place in depth in the homosexual man, deeper than the areas which could be controlled by the exercise of his will.

FL concluded his article by saying:

> To my readers who have more than an academic, more even than a pastoral, interest in this subject, but rather a personal one, I trust I have given some help and no offence.

Ten years later, in the 'Frank Lake Replies' series in *Renewal* magazine,[6] he took up the problem of a young man worried about the direction his sexuality was taking, and under pressure to join the homosexual community:

... First, about this emotive label, 'homosexual' – a lover of one's own sex, with erotic attraction as an adult, who is wholly or partly inhibited in loving persons of the opposite sex. We must recognize that, accurately used, it means many things at once, both 'good' and 'bad', healthy and sick, mature and immature, virtuous and sinful, constructive and destructive. To use it inaccurately, as a stereotype for a group of people who are to be exalted or abased, approved of, tolerated or 'knocked for six', only adds confusion and misunderstanding.

So, my friend (man or woman), don't be in a hurry to label yourself 'homosexual', with the implication that now you face life as such a one, 'up for grabs' by 'gay liberators' or 'down for disapproval' by the moralists. You are a human being sharing a common humanity, with a personal history unique to you. Because you are in Christ, a new and unique possibility of wholeness is opened up to you, in him. Don't settle for less. Wholeness in Christians isn't either 'sinless perfection' or 'perfect maturity' or 'perfect memory healing', as if we could in this life arrive at a state which made further radical developments and transformations meaningless ...

So, if the personality problem you're wrestling with is made up of fears of commitment to women, and a strangely compulsive need for commitment to men, with a deep fear of losing their friendship – and people want to call this 'homosexuality' or, as I prefer, 'andro-eroticism' – don't fear it. Accept it as part of the human base-line from which it is your task to work, with Father, Son, Holy Spirit and friends within and around you.

Healthy loving. It will help you to bear in mind certain facts. There is a positive, healthy love for one's own sex, based on a capacity for deep and intimate friendship between fathers and sons ... Cultural conditioning ... has attempted to eradicate this mutual tenderness between men. But where the Holy Spirit is at work, this fear-laden taboo on tenderness between men is lifted. A strong, wholly good love emerges . . .

Men who are scared of this normal, healthy aspect of homosexual tenderness are usually out of touch with the wholesome, nurturing feminine side of human nature. They are not able to be tender at all. Even if they marry, they remain afraid of the gentler emotions, terrified of not being 'masculine'. Their rejection of the tender aspects of loving, either towards men or women, is sick. The positive, deeply affectionate loving and holding of persons of one's own sex, without needing genital excursions, is entirely healthy . . . It is the genital aspect which easily gets out of proportion.

If you express this together without restraint, you raise questions of disobedience to the dynamic laws about the limits which God has given us 'for our own good always'. This teaching is consistent in both the Old and New Covenants. Jesus takes the command against adultery into the formerly secret areas of fantasy life. To use fantasy to conduct scenes of naked loving, whether of men or of women, which transgress this word of Christ's, is to put oneself into a position of rebellion against him. The way back from this is the joyful realism of penitence.

The cultural epidemic. I was going to use public opinion as the criterion for the acceptability or not of our secret fantasy life and the acted-out clandestine behaviour to which it often leads. But that is no longer a reliable criterion. What used to be 'shameful' is now 'shameless'. There are those who, 'knowing the judgement of God' on such affairs, 'not only do the same but have pleasure in those who do them' (Rom. 1:22). They now speak from within the bosom of the Church. Without censure they recommend the clubs, organizations and agencies in which homosexuals tend to become *mono*sexuals and are encouraged to engage in genital, oral and anal ways of arriving at orgasmic climax.

The argument is that between consenting adults no one is harmed. That is not true. What a man may claim is not harmful, only for so long as it is kept secret, is inevitably damaging to his integrity. He means and intends to be one thing in public and another in private. This is a harmful falsity. Those who do these things cannot expect the whole body of Christians to cut loose from the Scriptures and the Spirit's agelong and present advice that such behaviour is 'out of bounds', a trespass and an abomination, as, for instance, are adultery and fornication, just because they now find it hard to resist. For, whereas there is an aspect of homosexuality that is the love of persons of one's own sex

147

which is wholly creative, God-given, and deeply in touch with a rounded and healthy humanity, there is a pathological end to the homosexuality spectrum. It consists in the misogyny, the terror of, scorn of, aversion to, and cutting off of intimate and bonded affection, from the woman in the case of male homosexuals, and from the man in the case of female homosexuals. This is the twist. Its roots are readily traceable to traumatic events in the life of the infant.

It is a twist or deviation of the line of loving trust. Thank God you are only deviated, not decapitated. Many men have undergone a total blocking off of bodily loving. You are capable of loving, in the body, and with your body, at least one half of the human race. Thank God for that and take courage . . . The links in you from self to body are still intact.

So, my friend, beware of those who would counsel you from the homophile clubs to become monosexual, but beware equally of those churchmen who would counsel you out of the aridities of their schizoid fear of all the bodily life of persons. They forget Christ's constant affirmation of the goodness of appropriate touching and tender, loving holding. They choose to forget John, lying on Jesus's bosom at the great meal.

Beware, too, of the destructiveness of your own guilt feelings. You will tend to feel guilty anyway, whether you have acted on your homosexual feelings in genital ways, in fantasy or fact, all the way or not at all. The internalized parent or super-ego will threaten you mercilessly with disgrace and disaster for having 'broken this law' . . . This destructive internal self-castigation . . . can be endless. Stop that condemning voice at once, in Christ's name.

Continuing his reply in a further article,[7] he finishes with a few gentle words directed specifically at his questioner:

. . . this sexual problem is only one of dozens of similar problems which are part and parcel of being 'fallen' human beings. It is more difficult to live with than some others, but not as hard to shift in depth as yet other blocks which do not attract any social disapproval at all.

At your age, still in your early twenties, a lot can happen to move you towards a full human life as husband, father, and man of God, if that is what you are asking God to do in you . . .

Counselling and the Holy Spirit

RENEWAL IN THE HOLY SPIRIT

A new movement is springing up all around us, alongside, or at times uneasily within, the old conventional structures. Communities and groups are becoming established, of all manner of folks, throughout the English-speaking world and beyond it where Renewal has spread, groups in which there has been astonishing openness, in view of the Church's long record of closed and secretive defendedness within its congregations. It is the gathering together and increase of companies of people able to give to each other just those attitudes of openness, relaxed empathy, unhurried genuineness in listening, concrete helpfulness and effective 'being-alongside', which trained counsellors could be relied upon to give in one-to-one sessions . . .

When the whole once-painful business of sharing openly and frankly ceases to be a threatening prospect, but has become an occasion for breakthrough into a new and hitherto unimaginable universe of acceptance, the increase in ego-strength, derived from the mutual care of the fellowship, is immense.[1]

Frank Lake welcomed the movement towards Renewal in the Christian Churches for its openness to inner truth and genuine feeling. The Healing of the Memories had much in common with his own work. He was ever alert, however, to elements of self-deception and wishful thinking.

The Holy Spirit comes to us in what is, not in what ought to be. He enables us to speak about and to bear what is. Emotional things get quite unbearable if nobody dare to put into words what everybody's feeling. But if someone has the quiet courage to put into words what they are feeling, very often other people say, 'Thank you for putting it into words. I was trying to, but couldn't.'[2]

The upsurge of emotion among Christians spoke to him both of new opportunities and new responsibilities for the CTA. As early as 1973, he envisaged a need for further premises at Lingdale, to which people could come to work through experiences new to them. He wrote:[3]

We are increasingly being asked to help people who, in responding to the renewal of life in the Spirit which is moving in the Churches, have encountered disturbing experiences which are apt, by their local doctors and clergy, to be interpreted and treated repressively, as if they were 'nervous breakdowns'. This is not what they are.

They are experiences of the breakthrough of love and life into areas of experience which are normally kept walled off by cultural and religious demands merely for compliance to external codes of 'good' behaviour.

The influx of genuine love and energy is attempting to clean out the attics and cellars of the personality, and some painful and bewildering memories and experiences are thrown into the living room of consciousness. To equip Christian pastors and people to cope creatively, not destructively or depreciatingly, with these times of spiritual crises and transition is something to which we know we have been called. To have places where people could stay for a while during these painful but creative transitions would be a deep fulfilment of what we have been called upon to do through CTA. They could share for a while in the life of our community here and gain the understanding of these 'dark nights and troublesome days' which can integrate them into a maturing Christian character. These are 'childish things' which cannot be wisely put away by repressive measures. If men and women are to grow up into Christ in all things, his invitation to the children within us to come to him, for reconciliation and healing, not for crushing and obliteration, must be heard.

If this renewal is not to founder, as so many former renewals have done, in emotional immaturity, triumphalism, gnosticism, a reversion to rigorism or a variety of other avoidance reactions, we need places where the pain of growth and integration can be understood and validated. This must be done both for those in whom the changes are taking place and for their pastors and friends in Christ who need to stay alongside them with understanding and a new power of bearing . . .

Lingdale is placed at the heart of Nottingham's multiracial

community, largely unrelated to the splendid churches in our midst. I have had a burden about this for some months, particularly since I speak the language of our Pakistani immigrants. But beyond praying to be ready for something, we have few leads as to what this may mean.

> Further property was acquired and links were made with the styles of therapy and healing developed within the Renewal movement (as we saw in Chapter 7). In 1978 FL described the 'changing focus' of the Christian Church, which brought it closer to his own teaching:[4]

When we read the books which nurtured Reformed, Anglican and Catholic spiritual directors of only twenty years ago . . . we realize that their focus of interest was on conduct, on 'righteousness of life', as the power to avoid habitual sinning, to live the virtuous life, and 'to fulfil those good works which God had before ordained that we should walk in them'. In the last ten years, the Renewal in the Holy Spirit has changed that focus for many Christians to a more personal appropriation of the dynamic life of the indwelling Lord, with *more centredness in being than doing*, trusting than struggling, worshipping than working, not at all neglecting the second modality of 'works', but experiencing it as actually flowing out of the former . . . Gone is the old 'sin-counting', 'virtue-collecting', impersonal pattern . . .

This focus on being before doing is a New Testament change of emphasis, both for St Paul and for St John, who records Christ's own words to the disciples about the effect of the Holy Spirit's coming. When he, 'the Spirit of Truth', comes, 'he will convict the world of *sin*', not in the Pharisees' . . . sense of the word, of so many sins committed, but 'because they believe not on Me'.

Righteousness, too, changes its orientation; it is not even Christ's 'worthiness of life according to the law' that is the new righteousness, it is Christ's laying down his life and going through the obedience of death into the presence of the Father, there to intercede for his own, who will never again be collectors of righteousness in the old style.

Judgement, too, is overturned, from all its Old Testament canons, based on men's good deeds attracting God's favour . . . The New Testament man is no longer a 'stamp-collector' of impressive good works. He discovers (as Hans Küng quotes approvingly from Karl Barth) that 'It is not a mere figure of

151

speech to say that in faith man finds that the history of Jesus
Christ is his history . . . because his faith is a real apprehension
of his real being in Christ.'

> A paragraph in a later issue of *Contact* describes how the
> Holy Spirit empowers the counsellor to bear the pain of
> listening, whatever the temptation to evade or deny it:[5]

Our approach in Clinical Theology has been an act of faith in
wearing bifocal lenses as we counsel. Our experience is that,
looking penetratingly and listening intently to the affliction in
the heart of the human being, there opens up a situation that
is, in the end, and for all the more injured persons, a quite
intolerable affliction. The pain of it is such that our humanity
cannot bear the suffering. Splitting off and all the other defence
mechanisms then take over. At that moment, if we lift our eyes
a fraction and look through the longer-focus lens, we see Christ
Jesus, the Proper Man, in the central action of his life, which
was a Passion. We see him being the mediator who enables us
not to turn away in dread or disgust from what we first saw of
soul-shattering weakness and tribulation. The sight of him, in
the same extremity, enables us to move from the spectacle of the
one to the sight of the other, annealing the images, until the
Holy Spirit has effected a transformation, a reconciliation, a
peace, and the beginnings of praise.

> Elsewhere we find a warning against forced cheerfulness:[6]

It is regrettable that the Renewal has become associated in
people's minds with an unbalanced emphasis on the joy and
praise which well up from within. The same dynamic inflow of
the Holy Spirit's power, applying the work of Christ throughout
human personality, reaches as much into the depths as it does
into the heights, as much into the despairing heart as into the
dancing one. Among the ministry gifts, as the specific endow-
ment for a deeper ministry, there are those of wisdom, discernment, knowledge, prophecy, and inner healing. I think that
if these could be emphasized and their benefits more widely
experienced, much of the opposition to the renewal of charismata
would appropriately melt away.

Love, joy, and peace are all notably lacking in those who are
in states of breakdown. Nor is it sufficient to use the words to
evoke the emotions in those who are seriously lacking them.

What is characteristic about the Renewal, from the mental health viewpoint, is that the peace becomes palpable, the joy deeply felt, and the sense of love, God's fatherly love to us, the Son's dying love for those the Father had given him, and the Holy Spirit's gift of responsive love of unimagined intensity, abidingly real. This is central to anything the Church might have to offer in the future in the field of mental health.

There is a need for a deeper intellectual understanding of what the Spirit needs to and can work in us:[7]

... The 'Freudian revolution' has opened up for us ... the foundations of character in the perinatal traumas and our many-levelled reactions to them. Renewal prayer groups all over the world are finding that, through the ministry gifts of knowledge, discernment, and wisdom, the Holy Spirit is showing people that many of their mental illnesses and emotional blocks, with all that they have led to by way of reaction into misdirected living, are of perinatal origin. These sources of distorted perception, which 'war against the Spirit', stretch from conception through to the pre-verbal years, until our ordinary memory takes over. Retrieval of this dark continent of our ordinarily unconscious, or inaccessible, origins, shows how badly in need of evangelization this Christless world is.

All the foundations of our feelings about God and the Devil, Heaven and Hell, are here, but totally uninformed about the redemptive work of Christ. Yet, unless the God and Father of our Lord Jesus Christ was uninformed about these matters until the 20th century dawned on him, too, which is unlikely, God must have made provision in Christ for the redemption and renewal of human beings down to these depths.

No radical transformation of character is conceivable unless these twisted roots can be recognized, fully borne in their painfulness, and thoroughly put into context. This means being correctly connected up to sensations, emotions, and relationships which actually belong to repressed experiences before, during, and after birth; and also being put into the context of Christ's retrospective redemptive work in reconciling these innocent sufferers to the multiple bereavements and torture that accompanied their entry upon the human scene. The Suffering Servant identifies with, and carries, more than our culpable sins. He does this also for our weaknesses. We shall not emerge from mental sickness to mental health until we know experientially that these depth transformations not only can take place, but that they have been effected in us.

If the Renewal in the Holy Spirit is not to peter out in the bitterness of divided churches, and envious 'outsiders' who cannot or do not want to enter into a kind of 'joy' they suspect of being a strained euphoria, it must accept its mental health task, 'the renewing of the mind'. This healing of the memories means providing contexts of unconditional caring where hitherto 'competent' and 'strong' individuals can make contact with the tears, the weaknesses, the despairs, the longing, and the intolerable passivities and negativities that are battened down, but never at rest, in the cellars of primal memory.

Unless Christ is modelled here, by Christians ministering mutually to each other ... we will continue in our energy-consuming tensions and pursue our false goals religiously with hectic but misplaced enthusiasm.

In his later years, FL made a number of visits to Finland to lead seminars in Clinical Theology, arousing an interest which has since been maintained by the visits of the Revd Martin Yeomans. FL's last visit was at the invitation of Dr Martthi Paloheimo, who asked him to speak – not as a psychiatrist – about how to receive the Holy Spirit in the counselling situation. Many earlier passages, as well as those that follow, are from the tapescript of seminars during which he grappled with this assignment. The sessions were informal and unscripted and have had minor editing:

... this was a surprising request but it excited me a great deal. Last year I shared with you my researches in primal therapy. And, indeed, there is a very clear relationship in my mind between primal therapy and the Holy Spirit in counselling but this is a rather unusual coupling of subjects.[8]

Early on, he warned against a too-literal interpretation of Scripture:[9]

If St Paul came back and was standing here and we said to him, 'We have done very well, we have never said anything that you didn't say,' St Paul would say, 'Would you mind telling me what year you are speaking in?'
'Oh, we have just about reached 2000, Paul.'

154

COUNSELLING AND THE HOLY SPIRIT

'Two thousand years of living with the Holy Spirit and you don't know anything more than I said?'

'No, Paul, we are biblical Christians and we have never gone beyond what you said.'

'But didn't I write something about *anexichniastos*, the not-yet-searched-out richness of Christ? Did I not say that I had only just begun to understand? Did they never tell you that the Holy Spirit was going to guide the Church into all truth?'

Some time after the start of the seminars, he was still pleading with his audience for greater openness:

. . . We were talking about that passage [2 Cor. 3:14–18] about the veil that Moses put over his face. It is saying that Christ is the taking away of a veil . . . When Moses came down from the mountain he had to put a veil over his face because the glory was too strong. But then, it says in this passage . . . that he puts the veil over so that they shouldn't see that the splendour was fading. There is a big difference between putting a veil over your face to veil the splendour and putting a veil over your face because the splendour's gone. And yet, you see, that is the thing that quite often we are doing. In a very real sense we try sometimes to appear to be the same victorious Christians that we once were . . . You see this particularly in charismatic circles, where people have a certain fixed smile, which is said to be the appropriate smile for these circles . . .

He quotes from a textbook on how to run seminars in the Holy Spirit:

It says that the group leaders must be cheerful and smile pleasantly. That's rubbish. The only thing you want are leaders who are *real*. If I'm in a dark, deep place inside myself, I know people don't want to share my affliction, because my mother and my father said, 'Oh, stop it! You shouldn't be feeling like that.' Then I go deep inside myself into a lonely place. And I know, if they accept this smiling me, it isn't the real me. The glory has faded. But the closer you are to the Holy Spirit the more you can see in people's faces what they are trying to hide. There is a quality about the eyes and the mouth which even a smile won't disguise . . . Let us just be aware that there is this veil that people put over their faces for religious reasons . . .

155

He reads the passage and comments:

Do you see this very remarkable central verse here, verse 17? *The Lord is Spirit, and where the spirit of the Lord is, there is freedom.* As we keep looking at the face of Jesus Christ, and take the dishonest veil off our own faces, so that we really are looking at him and letting him see us, then what happens? It says that we are changed into his likeness from one degree of glory to another . . .

In a Newsletter, he wrote:[10]

Christian pastoral care can now, potentially, do more than merely trim the more rampant off-shoots of twisted behaviour. The root of the briar is laid bare. Our concept of the Holy Spirit's in-reach, in applying the reconciling work of Christ, as our fellow-sufferer and saviour, to the early sources of the trouble in man, cannot stand still, especially in this age which has witnessed the discovery of our once 'unconscious depths'. Either (as Freud and some Christians imply) this whole realm of our buried pains and passions belongs to 'the Devil', so that Christ is made to join the 'Parent', the 'powers that be', the 'super-ego' and our own fears of their return, in barring those unwanted selves from consciousness even more fiercely, or Christ fills all things by the penetration of his 'passionate', crucified love. He offers a belated welcome to our inner child of the past, recognizing that it suffered injustice and anguish even months before we were born. Christ came to free the oppressed, to set at liberty those who are bound. *It is inconceivable that the Father who sent the Son on this errand of self-disclosing rescue should have overlooked the bondage of 'unconscious' fear and pain. The Holy Spirit, bringing to bear the work of Christ, has now given to his Church the means to relieving the severest and most permanently damaging bonds of all, those tribulations which are imprinted so deeply on the minds, bodies and spirits of his little ones as to destroy their joy.*
. . . Society can only be changed, where it needs changing, by those who are themselves being changed where *they* need to be changed. The 'prejudice and ancient hurts' of inter-communal strife in various places are being healed, in so far as they are being healed at all, by men and women whose own deepest 'prejudices and ancient hurts' have first been exposed by the deep working of the Holy Spirit and been healed . . .

THE GIFTS OF THE SPIRIT

At several points in the Finland seminars FL spoke of the use of the gifts of the Spirit in counselling:[11]

. . . In 1 Cor. 14:2 St Paul says that tongues are to speak to God, not men. No one understands him when he is uttering mysteries in the Spirit. On the other hand, he who prophesies speaks to men for their upbuilding and their encouragement and consolation. Now I ask you, if you're a counsellor of somebody in trouble, what more could you wish than a gift that enables you to build people up solidly . . . to build up their strength and encourage them and, if they feel lonely and a bit on their own, to console them, to bring them together? And this is building from the ground up . . . if you're going to build somebody up you've got to start where the depths are. The building has to go right down to the foundations. If . . . there is no foundation in the depths . . . you're building castles in the air.

I was working in Vancouver a year or so ago, and there was a young pastor and his wife, and the pastor's wife was going into some very deep, dark places, and the Holy Spirit was helping her. And one day she went home with her husband and I realized that she was going to have a very deep and dark time. And her husband had to go out . . . so he left her some texts. And when he came back, she was still deep in this place and he kept mentioning a number of texts from Scripture that he thought might be helpful. For a while, being a very polite wife, she let him go on. Until, in sheer exasperation, she said, 'Stop flying paper aeroplanes over my head!' In other words, he was trying to build her up at the conscious level, while the Holy Spirit was working in depth for her right in the foundations . . .

Prophecy can be a helpful gift in counselling, but only if it speaks with great sensitivity to the depths. Tongues come from, and speak to, the depths, but are meaningless unless interpreted, when they become prophecy. True prophecy enables God to meet the hidden need in individual Christians:

. . . But there are many different layers of prophecy. The first step is to be present with somebody who is being counselled . . . And you realize that somebody is in a very difficult, bad place and they cannot hear God speaking at all, and you can't either.

You begin to share their depression. You begin to feel, 'Oh dear me, I wish they would stop!' Then you remind yourself that you've been given the Holy Spirit to go down into these places. And, frankly, almost the best prophetic word here is silence. People have told me that what they have valued most about a prayer group, or a counselling group, is their capacity to be present and silent.

One of the worst things that happens to a baby in infancy is to be left alone for long, long periods in silence. When people are strong enough to go into that silence, they stop chattering, they stop talking, and they say, 'I want to go into that primal silence.' If the Holy Spirit is giving us his empathy, then he is going to say, 'With those who are silent, be silent.'

It often helps to make it a comfortable, productive silence if you say just that. You see, if they are not looking at you they may think, 'Oh dear, he's/she's getting very uncomfortable because I'm not saying anything,' and they can't stand this silence. So, come to a distance which is near enough for them to feel that you are there. And then, put it into words: 'I'm aware that you've been taken into a deep, silent place. It's hard to bear the silence, but it's even harder if somebody starts talking. So please, let me just stay with you in the silence, sharing it with you.'

Now, in a very real sense, on a simple level, that is a godly understanding of where they are. And that's a word of wisdom. And that's a word of knowledge. And that's a word of prophecy. It's prophecy because it says that Christ can go into the silence, the deathly silence, with you. And, in Christ's name, I'm in that silence with you. That's a very healing thing.

Religious people, particularly, need a lot of faith just to shut up and not talk. I've known people to say afterwards, 'It was a miracle you didn't speak.' And it is also a very discerning thing to do.

And sometimes, when I'm for a long time with somebody who insists on being silent, I pray in tongues. They can't hear me, I'm not uttering anything, but I'm praying silently in tongues so that my mind will not wander or start working on other problems. So, you see . . . the Holy Spirit can give all the gifts of the Spirit, in a sense, in your wise silence.

But then, of course, out of this silence, it may be that the person really is seeking for a word. And it's quite likely that there will be two words. One word may be to put into words what you by the Spirit experienced – your experience of total loneliness. And they say, 'Yes, yes, I feel absolutely alone.' Now, if you leave it like that, it's a place of total despair, and the person could be tempted into what Kierkegaard calls *double despair*. To despair of the despairing self, and to destroy it.

And so, you are praying, 'Father, I don't want to fly any paper aeroplanes over this place, but I'm wondering whether you have any word to say into this place.' It's a word this person already knows, if they are a Christian. The Spirit can speak directly to them. So whatever you say must not come from you up on top here to them down below. What you say must come from alongside.

If you are free to utter this prophetic word, you could say something like this: 'Yes, I understand that you are experiencing total loneliness and the child in you knows only that. Yet I can hear the Christian person inside you speaking over the words of Christ, *I will never leave you nor forsake you.*' And they quietly answer, 'Yes, yes, that's right!' And so they have got hold of the two ends of the thing.

Of the gift of healing he has several things to say:[12]

Sometimes I get very troubled when some of my friends who are in the healing movement are presented with somebody who is suffering from cancer, or somebody who had some longstanding character disorder, and they say, 'All things are possible with God. Only believe and it will happen.'

Now that is true, but it worries me when I hear them saying it, because often they have no idea of the suffering and the waiting that is often necessary . . . Here we need the Holy Spirit's gift of knowledge and the gift of faith but, where faith comes as one of the long list of the gifts of the Spirit, it is a different sort of faith than that great big word of faith which begins the whole of our Christian life . . .

. . . What we are saying is that, yes, all things are possible for God, but the sovereignty of God determines in any given case whether it is good for this person or that to receive this or that kind of healing . . . [13]

Later on we find:

Healing is what the whole of counselling is really about, isn't it. Sometimes, in charismatic circles, they want to do the healing in isolation from all the other things. Their idea of healing is of something coming across that will send away, dismiss, and obliterate the whole of the pain in [an instant]. But that kind of thing is unworthy of the [Holy Spirit].

It may be necessary temporarily. There are some people who come to you who are in such anxiety that they have got no ego strength at all with which to bear it. I used to work with a Christian psychiatrist who, when he had patients like this, would say, 'You must let me carry your anxiety. I'll bear it for you and you will go free.' And they went away feeling free but he went home consumed with their anxiety. He felt that he was better able to deal with this anxiety than take it to Christ because for this person at this time it was rather [*premature*].

In the early days of a charismatic movement many people receive a kind of healing that is really only covering over all this. The problem that was causing anxiety was a deep, deep loneliness inside and the charismatic fellowship is so wonderful that you are miles away from this lonely place. The loneliness of infancy only reverberates up into consciousness when you are also lonely in consciousness. Since you are absolutely happy in this fellowship, there is no reason for this [anxious] stuff to come up at all.

However, since the Holy Spirit has a much deeper idea of healing than that, people find that, although in the fellowship as before, they still, strangely enough, feel lonely . . . Now is the time for deeper healing. Now is the time to take this journey with Christ deep into the depths, with your friends around you.[14]

On the gift of wisdom:

. . . The word wisdom is certainly something which, from time to time, you say as you are counselling. *Help me, Lord. I haven't the faintest idea what this is all about. I have no wisdom at all. Lord, give me wisdom.* And then, as you wait, suddenly something crops up and he says, 'Ask about that.' And then some wisdom comes in, something that you know is a wisdom that you would never have of yourself . . .

On the gift of knowledge:[15]

. . . Christian pastoral practice must be informed of the Holy Spirit's way of healing debilitating memories. Otherwise the 'credibility-gap' yawns too wide between the 'ought-to-be' and the 'actual'. The temptation to give up the strain of bridging the gap gets too strong. One side or the other gives way. Either pretended well-being loses its grip on the fact that it is pretence, or pretence collapses into the swirling eddies of chronic complaining.

Among those who have learned to use the gifts of the Spirit in 'Prayer Counselling', it has become a not uncommon occurrence to be given 'a word of knowledge' about the source of the prayed-for person's emotional bondage. For those whose 'sick' perception of themselves, humanly-speaking, as a waterless desert, or a root out of a dry ground, is in stark contrast with the Kingdom perceptions of themselves as one flowing with living water, 'the word of knowledge' frequently draws attention to the source of the dryness in the mother's inability to give any emotional vitality at all to her unborn child.

This word, of itself, spoken in the context of the confidence the person has gained in the Holy Spirit's authentic ministering word in the community of Faith, resonates down into the internal environment and 'makes good sense'. It interprets the person to himself or herself at the appropriate depth. The scientific physician in me is aware of the element of 'suggestion' here; but there is an adequate inbuilt corrective. People who have had several ministries of this sort are well able to distinguish between the 'word of knowledge' that does open doors in depth – so that data come trickling in, or flooding in, to confirm that interpretation – from the 'utterance' which owes too much to the ministering person's misplaced confidence in a 'word' that worked last time for someone else. The prayed-for person is totally open to testing out this interpretative key in all their cellar doors, but it opens none of them. Whenever 'words of knowledge' or 'prophetic gifts' are spoken of in Scripture, it is both with enthusiasm and reserve, with confidence and caution. But abuse does not ban right use. Abuses in the form of human intrusions and failings to hear and speak clearly from the Spirit's wisdom, do not invalidate the proper and continued use of these genuine gifts.

Our own practice is to begin, as always, with prayer for the Holy Spirit's guidance, and then to facilitate the person in *making their own search* into the prime occasions on which the feelings they are complaining of were felt with total intensity. Consistent deep breathing (so symbolic of the Spirit's fullness) enables the 'adult' to go down into these experiences which were overwhelming to the foetus or the baby without being overwhelmed or scared by them now . . .

On the gift of tongues:

. . . The general view now is that the gift of tongues is something which enables us to get into touch with all those important areas of life which, say, come before the age of three. You see, up to the age of three, both the right brain and the left brain have very primitive language. If you want to hear it, listen to [a toddler]. He's got a lot to say, and he says it very beautifully. And if you listen to him you know exactly what it is he is trying to say . . .

Now if God is concerned to recreate human beings from the depths, he has certainly got to start working below the . . . level of speech . . . Anybody I know who started to use tongues as a gift from the Holy Spirit would say, as I would say, that one thing it does do, it scrambles all the busy words and all the busy plans . . . and makes me deeply open . . . So what tongues seem to be doing is rescuing . . . rescuing this capacity for a deep, sympathetic intuition . . .

It's another way of becoming as little children. Don't let us make anything more serious about it than that.

Later he speaks of 'groanings that could not find words', and then concludes:

. . . The integration of personality that follows is tremendous. Because all the energy that was kept from other uses to push that stuff down, that energy is now free. So don't be afraid of tongues . . . [16]

As for discernment:

I've said a little about how speaking in tongues is valuable to get down into the pre-verbal elements of experience – into feelings like anger and grief. But why in this wonderful world do we need discernment? Well, we need discernment because the people in whom this is happening are still very human. Two things may happen when the Holy Spirit is working in this way. There is a potentially disruptive effect inevitable in the manifold gifts. They are so diverse that St Paul had to say time and again, *by the one spirit, by the one spirit, by the one spirit* . . .

People who are working here can begin to be disruptive. The boundaries of their own ego are not clear and they lose contact with what is going on in the fellowship. The Holy Spirit started them off with a very good trip, but they can sometimes stay with their own private trip and someone has to be exercising discernment . . .

The other thing is that there are many people in the Church who would suppress all the gifts of the Spirit . . . with the result that all the Holy Spirit's rich variety never gets through to people . . . The assumption of the preacher is that *what I say is good for everybody and everybody goes away from listening to me believing and thinking the same thing.* There is no diversity and only one person is allowed to speak, so that all the gifts of the Spirit that are richly present for the healing of individuals are completely suppressed.

So the task of discernment is to see where too much divisiveness is happening, but also to validate some of the strange individual journeys that have to be made.

Discernment may also be needed to disentangle the emotions of group members. FL drew attention to the gift of one of the fellowship to feel what others were feeling, to weep with people and help them to get in contact with their pain:

. . . But anybody who has this sort of gift has often got a lot of pain in themselves . . . And you don't always know what pain belongs to the person and what belongs to you. When you were helping someone in the prayer meeting, R., I didn't know whether you were helping or being helped. And so, I said, 'Hey . . . I must discern what is going on. Let me have a look at your faces.' You were five people all in a chain of grief and my task was to discern who was doing what to whom.

This is part of the task of discernment: to try and find out what really belongs to the person being helped and what belongs to the helper. Any of you familiar with counselling and supervision know that this is the task of supervision.[17]

WHICH BRINGS US TO WHERE WE BEGAN

It is well to remind ourselves that the power of the Spirit was nothing new, had been fundamental to Clinical Theology from the beginning. In 1967, FL said that Christ's presence closes up the split 'caused by dread in man's whole individual social and spiritual being' by bearing the pain:[18]

We must now ask, by whom was this atoning, reconciling activity mediated between God the Father and God the Son, from Gethsemane to Golgotha. By whom, also, will it be made applicable to us, who believe ourselves to be, by his grace, elected to sonship and called to the same pastoral office, to lay down our lives for the sheep, freed from the fear of dying so that they can live in freedom. It is, of course, the Holy Spirit, whose incognito has been so well preserved, who does not draw attention to himself, but is promised to those who ask for him.

We must now speak of the Holy Spirit . . . claiming Christ's victory in the realm of the demonic powers, the archetypal destroyers, and the individual afflictions which stem from our flight from dread. The power of consciousness . . . cannot reach these elusive enemies. But they can be reached, overcome, turned round in their tracks, and made to join the triumphal procession of Christ, only by the power of the groaning Holy Spirit – his, and ours in him.

He also spoke of:

. . . the fear we all have of the unconscious. We are afraid to lift the lid of Pandora's box. Nor are we, as Christians, in general required to do this. But, when the waters break over us, we are, as the Psalmist was, called to be aware of, and co-operate with, the sanctifying Holy Spirit, when he is cleansing us in depth in the night season . . .

The Holy Spirit is waiting to evangelize this dark continent. If he does not, our whole civilization may well be doomed. If, by Christians and the Church, he is allowed to heal the deep cleavages within us, holiness is possible and community is possible, but not otherwise.

In *Mutual Caring*, it is put differently:[19]

So, the way back to Christ, to inner integrity, and to membership of the forgiven, reconciled, responsible, open and fully sharing Body of Christ, the return to the community that cannot call itself conventional, but can identify itself as characteristically Christian, must be through the recovery of memory . . .

Frank Lake died in the spring of 1982, of an inoperable cancer. Struggling to get said all that he had to say, he continued writing to the end. Among his last written words were these addressed to his followers in the Holy Spirit:[20]

Keep close to Christ, as the person whose life within you is the source of all the creative activity that has an eternally-lasting quality. Keep close to the Body of Christ, the Christian family. Build up its life from depths examined and purified in these new ways.[21] It has potentialities for growth within itself and for a service of healing in the wider community in the years ahead that is unprecedented in its depth and outreach.

Shortly before his death, he was interviewed on BBC radio by Rosemary Hartill. He summarized his conclusions about the lasting power of emotional experiences in the mother's womb on people's perception of themselves. Towards the end, Rosemary Harthill asked whether he was at all frightened of dying. His instant response was, 'Good gracious, no. No . . . I have the sense that Christ is so real . . . his timing is so perfect . . . I know that when my time comes, it is the perfect moment, the perfect day . . .'

He told her that he had necessarily been discussing his ideas with her. 'But when you've gone, I shall say, "Lord Jesus, come in and fill every cell of my body with your gentle peace . . . And take me at another pace. This cerebral pace is too fast . . ." '

Returning to ideas for a moment and giving a little chuckle, he added: 'The funny thing is . . . often what people fear about their death is that it will be too like their birth . . .' His own birth, he said, seemed to have been 'relatively untraumatic'.

He described death as 'going on into God. I've got a great sense that we shall be just beginning to know about God . . . I've been a great person for knowing *about* things. And now my task is to know them directly, to encounter God in a more direct way, because that's going to be the mode of activity on the other side . . .'

The interview ended with Frank uttering a very soft, speculative, anticipatory 'Mmmmmm . . .'

At the time of his death, it seemed to many that Frank Lake had gone too far in suggesting that our most ineradicable character patterns were already being laid down in the three months after our conception. His enthusiasm for primal work seemed to them excessive. Yet, a year later,

165

the first International Congress on Pre- and Peri-natal Psychology was held, showing that he did not, after all, stand alone. Once again, let us allow him the last word. In this passage he was writing about earlier 'excesses' which had, by the time of his death, lost much of their power to affront or amaze. He was surely entitled to claim for himself the quality of 'prophetic intemperance':[22]

Pastoral care is a matter of temperance. 'The fruit of the Spirit is temperance.' 'Every man who strives for mastery is temperate in all things.' My former supervisor in psychotherapy, Dr Ronald Markillie, in reviewing my book, found it 'intemperate' and I concede the fairness of that criticism. It was made by a man who stood in the centre and saw me as way off-centre.

There is (and has been in myself) a neurotic intemperance, as when our being 'terribly keen on this', or 'awfully sure about that', or 'dreadfully determined to get this done', are all indicative of a flight into activity, away from intolerable passivities within ourselves which we cannot, or will not, face up to in consciousness.

There is, however, a prophetic kind of intemperance which is the handmaid of temperance. It sees a state of affairs which has run to excess in one direction and sets out to counter it, for a limited period of time, in the opposite direction. It may itself be, temporarily, excessive.

As Kierkegaard's niece, Henrietta Lund, wrote of him: *One-sidedness, yes, that is the indictment; but we must remember that, without a vigorous one-sidedness, things are seldom put right* . . .

Notes

INTRODUCTION: CLINICAL THEOLOGY IN CONTEXT

1. Lake, F., *Clinical Theology*. Darton, Longman and Todd 1966.
2. *Pastoral Care and the Training of Ministers*. British Council of Churches/Institute of Religion and Medicine 1968.
3. Freud, S. and Pfister, O., *Psychoanalysis and Faith*. Hogarth Press 1963.
4. McKenzie, J. G., *Souls in the Making: An Introduction to Pastoral Psychology*. George Allen and Unwin 1928.
5. Weatherhead, L. D., *Psychology, Religion and Healing*. Hodder and Stoughton 1951.
6. Guntrip, H., *Psychology for Ministers and Social Workers*. George Allen and Unwin, 3rd Edition, 1971.
7. Fairbairn, W. R. D., *Psychoanalytic Studies of the Personality*. Tavistock 1952.
8. Melinsky, M. A. H., 'Clinical Theology: a survey', *Religion and Medicine*. SCM 1970, p. 119.
9. Ibid., p. 127.
10. *Contact: The Interdisciplinary Journal of Pastoral Studies*, 74 (1982: 1).
11. Lake, F., *Tight Corners in Pastoral Counselling*. Darton, Longman and Todd 1981.
12. Peters, J., *Frank Lake, the Man and his Work*. Darton, Longman and Todd 1989.
13. *Pre- and Peri-Natal Psychology*, The Journal of the Pre- and Peri-Natal Psychology Association of North America (first published 1987); *The International Journal of Prenatal and Perinatal Studies*, The Journal of The International Society of Prenatal and Perinatal Psychology and Medicine (first published 1989).

CHAPTER 1 CLINICAL THEOLOGY

1. Darton, Longman and Todd, London 1966, p. xii. A shorter version of the book, abridged by Martin H. Yeomans and also called *Clinical Theology*, was first published in 1986.
2. Ibid., p. 15.
3. Ibid., pp. 1159–60.
4. 'What is Clinical Theology?', tapescript, 8 Dec. 1966, p. 2.

5. Whereas in the previous excerpt Dr Lake was writing, under the chapter heading 'Paranoid and related conditions', of the type of person who dares not admit to any weakness or need of help, here he is using his characteristic phrase for the depths of despair into which a person may be plunged whose defenses are primarily of the schizoid type, and who feels cut off from any possibility of loving relationships.
6. 'The Clinical Theology Association, History and Development', a report (1973).
7. 15 April, 1965. Michael Hare Duke was a Pastoral Director of CTA from 1962 to 1964, and a Pastoral Consultant from 1964 to 1969, when he was appointed Bishop of St Andrews, Dunkeld and Dunblane.
8. By 1990 the number of clergy and lay people had reached well over 20,000.
9. Sylvia Lake takes issue with this, saying, 'God's ability to give us his own Life does not in the last resort depend on the will of man at all. His will unaided by ours brings us to new birth in places as hidden as the womb itself.'
10. *Listening*.
11. *Clinical Theology*, p. xix.
12. In an Appendix to E. N. Ducker's *A Christian Therapy for a Neurotic World*, George Allen & Unwin 1961, for which FL also wrote the Foreword.
13. *Contact*, 88 (1985): 3.
14. *Clinical Theology*, p. 138.
15. Post Green tapescript, pp. 74–76.
16. Op cit., Note 4, pp. 10–11.
17. *Mutual Caring*, TS, Part 2, p. 12. FL worked on this book-length manuscript at intervals during his last illness. Uneven in quality and (it seems to me) intention, it remains so far unpublished, but contains lively passages and, in places, sums up his later thinking.
18. In a famous experiment, the Russian physiologist Pavlov trained, or 'conditioned', dogs to salivate at the sound of the bell which was rung at feeding time, whether or not food appeared. If, however, the dogs were disappointed too often, they would eventually slink to the far side of their cages at the sound of the bell, even if the food was brought to them.

CHAPTER 2 MENTAL HEALTH

1. *Personal Identity – Its Origin*, Lingdale Paper 6, p. 3.
2. *Clinical Theology*, 1966, *Tight Corners in Pastoral Counselling*, 1981, and *With Respect*, 1982, all from Darton, Longman and Todd.
3. In the TS of a 172 page article called 'Theological issues in mental health for India' (1978), p. 1. Commissioned by the Institute for

the Study of Religion and Society in Bangalore but apparently never published.

4. Ibid., p. 33.
5. Ibid., p. 49.
6. Ibid., pp. 52–7.
7. Ibid., p. 78.
8. In his Presidential address to New College Theological Society, Edinburgh on 'The bearing of our knowledge of the unconscious on the theology of evangelism and pastoral care', p. 22.
9. TS (1971), pp. 1–2. Later published as 'The emotional health of the clergy', *The Epworth Review*, 1:2 (May 1974), pp. 38–49.
10. See the submissions from members of his family in John Peters's *Frank Lake, the Man and his Work*, Darton, Longman and Todd 1989.
11. Op. cit., Note 3, pp. 120–3.
12. Third Programme of the BBC (18 July 1967), in the series 'Secular Christianity'.
13. Newsletter 10 (1968).
14. 'The basic aim of medical missions', *The Christian Graduate*, 5:1 (1952).
15. Lingdale Paper 2 (1986), pp. 5–15.
16. *Mutual Caring*, p. 7.
17. 'Reflection on development and change in the Clinical Theology Association, 1964–1975', *Contact*, 50 (1975:3), pp. 8–13.
18. Op. cit., Note 3, p. 23.
19. I take him to mean that, by reason of our adaptation to society, each one of us has denied the basic innermost truth about ourselves. Cf. opening paragraph of Ch. 4.
20. Op. cit., Note 3, p. 35.

CHAPTER 3 THE ORIGINS OF MENTAL AND SPIRITUAL ANGUISH

1. *The Origin and Development of Personal Identity*, CT pamphlet 4, Foreword by Frank Lake.
2. 'Theological issues in mental health for India', pp. 6–7.
3. *Mutual Caring*, p. 127.
4. 'Primal integration work', *Contact*, 58 (1978:1).
5. Op. cit., Note 2, p. 29.
6. Op. cit., Note 3, pp. 23 and ff.
7. Op. cit., Note 2, p. 99.
8. Op. cit., Note 3, Part 2, p. 25.
9. Post Green tapescript, pp. 52 and ff.
10. Ibid., pp. 75–6.
11. Op. cit., Note 3, p. 57.
12. Darton, Longman and Todd 1981, p. vii.
13. 'Research into the prenatal aetiology of mental illness, personality and psychosomatic disorders', written by Frank Lake on behalf of the Research Section of the Clinical Theology Association.

14. Dr Roger Moss, at the request of the Clinical Theology Association, conducted a follow-up survey of more than 500 participants at workshops at Lingdale, Nottingham. 274 responded. The research shows links between 'memories' and birth histories previously unknown to the subject; a wealth of material shedding light on foetal life, particularly when under stress; and a great deal of personal growth and benefit obtained from the integrating process experienced at the workshops. The methods and implications of this work are described fully in a forthcoming book.
15. Op. cit., Note 3, p. 34.
16. Ibid., p. 46.
17. Op. cit., Note 2, p. 97.
18. Ibid., p. 20.
19. Ibid., p. 19.
20. *Self and Society*, 6:7 (July 1978), in an interview with Alix Pirani on 'The significance of perinatal experience'.
21. Roger Moss comments: The issue of cellular memory is a topic of continuing interest. Frank Lake related it to circulating catecholamines. Since his death, the concept has been pursued further. As yet, nobody has found convincing ways to prove it, and it may take a long time before there will be any suitable techniques to do so other than indirectly. Thus, basically, it currently has the status of no more than an hypothesis, but at least provides a credible mechanism to explain some of the material uncovered in psychotherapeutic work.
22. *Contact*, 68 (1980:3), p. 11.
23. Dr Roger Moss, at the request of CTA, has been evaluating the clinical evidence accumulated by FL. His findings are still to be published.
24. Lingdale Paper 2, pp. 13–14.
25. Address to New College Theological Society (cf. Ch. 2, Note 8), pp. 19–21.

CHAPTER 4 THE DEFENCE OF THE PERSONALITY – PART I

1. 'Theological issues for mental health in India', p. 118.
2. Address to New College Theological Society (cf. Ch. 2, Note 8), pp. 33–4.
3. 'I don't want to feel angry but I do', *Renewal*, 59 (Oct/Nov 1975).
4. 'Power to throw away', *Renewal*, 60 (Dec 1975/Jan 1980).
5. *Clinical Theology*, p. 380.
6. Todd, A., *The Hysterical Personality Pattern*, pp. 3–4.
7. Post Green tapescript, p. 157.
8. Finland tapescript, p. 113.
9. Op. cit., Note 6, p. 6.
10. Op. cit., Note 2, p. 7.
11. Ibid., p. 31.

12. 'A deeper understanding of "Affliction" ', 2:2 (May 1980).
13. Op. cit., Note 2, p. 34.
14. Op. cit., Note 7, p. 124.

CHAPTER 5 THE DEFENCE OF THE PERSONALITY – PART II

1. 2nd impression, inside front cover.
2. Ibid., inside back cover.
3. Finland tapescript, pp. 89–120.
4. Post Green tapescript, pp. 167–8.
5. Ibid., p. 89.
6. Transcript of talk delivered on 18 September 1965, p. 1.
7. Ibid., p. 14.
8. Ibid., pp. 19–20.
9. *Contact*, 20 (April 1967), p. 2.
10. Ibid., p. 4.
11. 'I just feel worthless', *Renewal*, 67 (Feb/March 1977).
12. A counselling term derived from the work of Carl Rogers.
13. Op. cit., Note 4, p. 77.

CHAPTER 6 CLINICAL THEOLOGY AND OTHER THERAPIES

1. *Tight Corners in Pastoral Counselling*. Darton, Longman and Todd, London, 1981, p. 12.
2. Rogers, C., *On Becoming a Person*. Constable 1964.
3. *Towards Effective Counselling and Psychotherapy*. Chicago, Aldine, 1967.
4. 'Theological issues in mental health for India', p. 93.
5. The term FL seems to have settled for in his own work is 'Primal Integration', which stresses not only the recovery of primal sensations and 'memories', but the use of them to make sense of hitherto inexplicable problems in adult life. This also avoids legal difficulties with Janov, who states in all his books that 'Primal Therapy' may only be practised by the people authorized by him.
6. Op. cit., Ch. 3, Note 19.
7. *Contact*, 58 (1978:1). In this issue he lists the wide range of therapies which had contributed to his own thinking.
8. 'Re-evaluation counselling', by Colin Davison, 'Prayer counselling', by Ian Davidson and 'Bioenergetics', by Geoffrey Whitfield.
9. Janov, A., *The Primal Scream*. Putnam, N.Y., 1970.
10. FL later makes specific reference to Rank's *The Trauma of Birth*, Harper Torchbooks, N.Y., 1934, and Nandor Fodor's *The Search for the Beloved*, University Books, N.Y., 1949.
11. *Games People Play*. Penguin 1964.
12. Perls *et. al.*, *Gestalt Therapy*. Dell, N.Y., 1965.
13. The book of that name is by T. A. Harris, Pan Books 1973.
14. From the incomplete typescript for a lecture which appears, from internal evidence, to date from 1975.
15. Members of CTA were, and remain, divided as to whether such

competence can be claimed. Many feel that his own remarkable results, though apparently simply achieved, owed much to his personality, training and long experience of work at the depths of the personality.

16. 'The work of Christ in the healing of primal pain', *Theological Renewal*, 6. Published with *Renewal*, 69 (June/July 1977). Reprinted as an Appendix to Peters's *Frank Lake, the Man and his Work*, Darton, Longman and Todd 1989.

17. *Mutual Caring*, p. 56.

18. 'The neurological basis of primal integration theory', a 32 page paper dating from the late 70s, of which the final pages are missing. Extracts are taken from pp. 1–15.

CHAPTER 7 THE COUNSELLING MINISTRY

1. Reference is made to FL's Appendix to this book in Ch. 1, Note 11.
2. Dr Michael Balint of the Tavistock Clinic.
3. 'The threatened nervous breakdown', Part 1, *The Expository Times*, LXXVIII: 9, p. 264.
4. In which he acknowledges his indebtedness to Howard Clinebell's *Basic Types of Pastoral Counselling*, Abingdon Press, N.Y., 1966.
5. 'Hope in the clinical setting', *Contact*, 34 (February 1971), p. 18.
6. Newsletter 19, pp. 4–5.
7. Ibid., pp. 7–8.
8. See R. R. Carkhuff, *Helping and Human Relations*. Holt, Rhinehart and Winston, N.Y., 1969.
9. *The Expository Times*, LXXVIII: 9 (June 1967) and 10 (July 1967).
10. Newsletter 7, 1966.

CHAPTER 8 SEXUALITY AND SPIRITUALITY

1. Given in Great Saint Mary's Church, and published together with lectures by Howard Root ('Love, law and liberty') and V. A. Demant ('Chastity and charity') and an Introduction by Hugh Montefiore, by Hodder & Stoughton as *We Must Love One Another or Die*, 1966.
2. One of a series of lectures on Morality and Religion given in the Chapel of St John's College, 2 November 1969.
3. Op. cit., Note 2.
4. Sylvia Lake, not wanting readers to be misled by this paragraph taken out of context, suggests, 'This passage is a dangerous view unless it is made quite clear that the law is substituted by Christ's own love in us for the other person – only then can the law be laid aside. And who of us loves with such wholeness and purity?

Therefore we need the law to guide us. We need to embrace its guarding of us until we are freed from human selfishness and enabled to love with the love that Christ expressed and lived out, for us to see and understand.'

5. Part of the series called 'First aid in counselling', *The Expository Times*, LXXVIII: 12 (Sept. 1967).
6. 'Same-sex loving', Part 1, *Renewal*, 62 (Apr/May 1976).
7. Ibid., Part 2, *Renewal*, 63 (Jun/Jul 1976).

CHAPTER 9 COUNSELLING AND THE HOLY SPIRIT

1. *Mutual Caring*, p. 4.
2. Finland tapescript, p. 71.
3. Newsletter 20 (November 1973), p. 6.
4. 'The newer therapies', *Contact*, 58 (1978: 1) p. 11.
5. 'The theology of pastoral counselling', *Contact*, 68 (1980: 3), p. 2.
6. 'Theological issues for mental health in India', p. 47.
7. Ibid., pp. 171–2.
8. Finland tapescript, p. 1.
9. Ibid., p. 23.
10. *Clinical Theology News*, Report No. 1 (Dec. 1978), p. 3.
11. Finland tapescript, pp. 128–31.
12. Ibid., p. 30.
13. Ibid., p. 136.
14. Ibid., p. 134.
15. Op. cit., Note 10, p. 2.
16. Finland tapescript, pp. 79–83.
17. Ibid., pp. 137–9.
18. 'The bearing of our knowledge of the unconscious on the theology of evangelism and pastoral care', p. 26 and ff.
19. *Mutual Caring*, p. 86.
20. Ibid., Introduction, p. 7.
21. Presumably the ways described in his MS of recovering intra-uterine memories in the context of a Christian group.
22. Op. cit., Note 3, p. 1.

Index

174